"A HILARIOUS PRIMER OF INSTANT COOKING DELICACIES"

—LIFE

"The genesis of this book was a luncheon with several good friends, all of whom hate to cook but have to. At that time, we were all unusually bored with what we had been cooking and, therefore, eating. For variety's sake, we decided to pool our ignorance, tell each other our shabby little secrets, and toss into the pot the recipes we swear by instead of at.

"These recipes have not been tested by experts. That is why they are valuable. Experts in their sunny spotless test kitchens can make anything taste good. But even we can make these taste good."

—PEG BRACKEN

Other Fawcett Crest Books by
    Peg Bracken:

The I Hate to Housekeep Book
I Try to Behave Myself
Appendix to the I Hate to Cook Book

The
I Hate to Cook
Book

by Peg Bracken

DRAWINGS BY HILARY KNIGHT

A Fawcett Crest Book

Fawcett Publications, Inc., Greenwich, Conn.

Dedicated,
with mixed emotions,
to
Constance Averill McCready,
who got me into this,
and helped get me out

Contents

Introduction

Some women, it is said, like to cook.

This book is not for them.

This book is for those of us who hate to, who have learned, through hard experience, that some activities become no less painful through repetition: childbearing, paying taxes, cooking. This book is for those of us who want to fold our big dishwater hands around a dry Martini instead of a wet flounder, come the end of a long day.

When you hate to cook, life is full of jolts: for instance, those ubiquitous full-color double-page spreads picturing what to serve on those little evenings when you want to take it easy. You're flabbergasted. You wouldn't cook that much food for a combination Thanksgiving and Irish wake. (Equally discouraging is the way the china always matches the food. You wonder what you're doing wrong; because whether you're serving fried oysters or baked beans, your plates always have the same old blue rims.)

And you're flattened by articles that begin "Of course you know that basil and tomatoes are soulmates, but *did* you know

. . ." They can stop right there, because the fact is you didn't know any such thing. It is a still sadder fact that, having been told, you won't remember. When you hate to cook, your mind doesn't retain items of this nature.

Oh, you keep on buying cookbooks, the way a homely woman buys hat after hat in the vain hope that this one will do it. And, heaven knows, the choice is wide, from the *haute cuisine* cookbook that is so *haute* it requires a pressurized kitchen, through Aunt Em's Down-on-the-Farm Book of Cornmeal Cookery, all the way to the exotic little foreign recipe book, which is the last thing you want when you hate to cook. Not only are there pleasanter ways to shorten your life, but, more important, your husband won't take you out for enchiladas if he knows he can get good enchiladas at home.

Finally, and worst of all, there are the big fat cookbooks that tell you everything about everything. For one thing, they contain too many recipes. Just look at all the things you can do with a chop, and aren't about to! What you want is just one little old dependable thing you can do with a chop besides broil it, that's all.

Also, they're always telling you what any chucklehead would know. "Place dough in pan to rise and cover with a clean cloth," they say. What did they *think* you'd cover it with?

This terrible explicitness also leads them to say, "Pour mixture into 2½ qt. saucepan." Well, when you hate to cook, you've no idea what size your saucepans are, except big, middle-sized, and little. Indeed, the less attention called to your cooking equipment the better. You buy the minimum, grudgingly, and you use it till it falls apart. If anyone gives you a shiny new cooking utensil for Christmas, you're as thrilled as a janitor with a new bucket of cleaning solvent.

But perhaps the most depressing thing about those big fat cookbooks is that you have to have one. Maybe your mother-in-law gives you a bushel of peppers or a pumpkin, and you must make piccalilli or a pumpkin pie. Well, there's nothing to do but look it up in your big fat cookbook, that's all. But you certainly can train yourself not to look at anything else.

Now, about this book: its genesis was a luncheon with several good friends, all of whom hate to cook but have to. At that time, we were all unusually bored with what we had been cooking and, therefore, eating. For variety's sake, we decided to pool our ignorance, tell each other our shabby little secrets, and toss into the pot the recipes we swear by instead of at.

This is an extension of the result. It is seasoned with a good sprinkling of Household Hints (the *crème de la crème* of a private collection of 3,744). Mainly, though, it contains around two hundred recipes.

These recipes have not been tested by experts. That is why they are valuable. Experts in their sunny spotless test kitchens can make anything taste good. But even *we* can make these taste good.

Their exact origins are misty. Some of them, to be sure, were off-the-cuff inventions of women who hate to cook and whose motivating idea was to get in and out of that kitchen fast. But most of them were copied from batter-spattered file cards belonging to people who had copied them from other batter-spattered file cards, because a good recipe travels as far, and fast, as a good joke. So, in most cases, it is impossible to credit the prime source, although the prime source was probably a good cook who liked to.

Bless her, and bow low. We who hate to cook have a respect bordering on awe for the Good Cooks Who Like to Cook— those brave, energetic, imaginative people who can, and do, cook a prime rib and a Yorkshire pudding in a one-oven stove, for instance, and who are not frightened by rotisseries. But we've little to say to them, really, except, "Invite us over often, please." And stay away from our husbands.

And, if you hate to cook, expect no actual magic here, no Escoffier creations you can build in five minutes or even ten. But you might well find some recipes you'll like—to use the word loosely—to make now and again. Perhaps you'll even find some you will take to your heart. At the very least, you should find a hands-across-the-pantry feeling, coming right through the ink. It is always nice to know you are not alone.

Chapter 1

30 Day-by-Day Entrees

or The Rock Pile

NEVER DOUBT it, there's a long, long trail a-winding, when you hate to cook. And never compute the number of meals you have to cook and set before the shining little faces of your loved ones in the course of a lifetime. This only staggers the imagination and raises the blood pressure. The way to face the future is to take it as Alcoholics Anonymous does: one day at a time.

This chapter contains recipes for thirty everyday main dishes. Some of them aren't very exciting. In fact, some are pretty dull—just as a lot of recipes are in the other cookbooks, but the other cookbooks don't admit it. And some of the recipes in this chapter are so—well, so simple —that they'd have any *cordon bleu* chef pounding his head with his omelet pan.

The thing about these recipes is this: they're *here!* You don't have to ferret them out of your huge, jolly, encyclopedic cookbook. *And they'll get you through the month!*

After all, who needs more than thirty recipes? You already have your own standard routines: the steak-roast-and-chop bit, the frozen-TV-dinner bit, the doctored-up-canned-beans bit, not to mention your mother's favorite recipe for Carrot-Tapioca-Meat Loaf Surprise. And if somebody waves a dinner invitation, you leap like a trout to the fly. So, with these additional thirty, you're in.

Now, the points that are special about them are these:

1. They all taste good.

2. They are all easy to make.

3. Each has been approved by representative women who hate to cook, and not one calls for a *bouquet garni.*

4. Some do two jobs. They involve either meat, fish, or chicken plus a vegetable, so all you need is bread of some kind, or meat, fish, or chicken and a starch, so all you need is a vegetable.

5. Many can be made ahead. (Of course, you won't do this very often. When you hate to cook, you keep postponing it. But once in a while, you wake up full of fire. This is the time when you can lump dinner right in with the other dirty work you do around the house in the morning, and get it *done.*)

6. Most of them are quick to fix. Actually, you can't trust the word "quick" any more. Some cookbooks, when they say "quick," mean that you needn't grind your own flour. Others mean that you can pour a can of tomato soup over a veal chop and call it Scallopini.

We must face facts. If a recipe calls for eleven different chopped ingredients and cream sauce and a cheese-topped meringue, you don't call it "quick" if you hate to cook. On the other hand, that tomato soup on the veal chop will taste remarkably like tomato soup on a veal chop, and you can't call it Scallopini.

The really jet-propelled recipes in this book are in Chapter 11. But here we take a middle-of-the-road path. Thawing and/or cooking time isn't what bothers you most when you hate to cook; it's preparation time, which, in these recipes, is mercifully short. For instance:

SWEEP STEAK

4-6 *servings*

(*So-called because a couple of seasons ago this recipe swept the country.*)

2- to 3-pound round steak or pot roast
package of onion-soup mix

Put the meat on a sheet of aluminum foil big enough to wrap it in. Sprinkle the onion-soup mix on top of it, fold the foil, airtight, around it, put it in a baking pan, and bake it at 300° for three hours or 200° for nine hours, it really doesn't matter. You can open it up, if you like, an hour or so before it's done, and surround it with potatoes and carrots.

STAYABED STEW

5-6 servings

(*This is for those days when you're en negligee, en bed, with a murder story and a box of bonbons, or possibly a good case of flu.*)

Mix these things up in a casserole dish that has a tight lid:

2 pounds beef stew meat, cubed
1 can of little tiny peas *
1 cup of sliced carrots
2 chopped onions
1 teaspoon salt, dash of pepper

1 can cream of tomato soup thinned with ½ can water (or celery or mushroom soup thinned likewise)
1 big raw potato, sliced
piece of bay leaf *

Put the lid on and put the casserole in a 275° oven. Now go back to bed. It will cook happily all by itself and be done in five hours.

Incidentally, a word here about herbs and seasonings. These recipes don't call for anything exotic that you buy a box of, use once, and never again. Curry powder, chili powder, oregano, basil, thyme, marjoram, and bay leaf are about as far out as we get. And if your family says, "What makes it taste so funny, Mommie?" whenever you use any herbs at all, you can omit them (although if you omit chili from chili or curry from curry, you don't have much left, and you'd really do better to skip the whole thing).

But as a rule, don't hesitate to cut the amount of a seasoning way down, or leave it out, when it's one you know you don't like. This goes for green pepper, pimento, and all that sort of thing, too. (I mention this only because we ladies

---

* If you don't like this, leave it out.

who hate to cook are easily intimidated by recipes and recipe books, and we wouldn't dream of substituting or omitting; we just walk past that particular recipe and never go back again.)

We must assert ourselves. I, by way of example, think rosemary is for remembrance, not for cooking, and the amount of rosemary I have omitted from various recipes would make your head swim. The dishes turned out quite all right, too.

PEDRO'S SPECIAL

3 ample servings

(Very easy; very good with beer; good even without it.)

1 pound ground round steak
1 chopped onion
1 garlic clove, minced
1 can tomato sauce plus ⅓ can tomato juice, consommé, or water

1 ordinary pound can kidney or chili beans with liquid
¼ teaspoon oregano
2 tablespoons chili powder
1 can or bag corn chips
a bit of lettuce
more chopped onion

Brown together, in a little oil, the ground meat, onions, and garlic. Stir in the tomato sauce, oregano, and chili powder. Now dust off a good-sized casserole, grease it, and alternate layers of this mixture with layers of beans and corn chips, ending with corn chips. Bake it, covered, at 350° for forty-five minutes, and uncover it for the last ten. Before you serve it, strew some shredded lettuce and chopped raw onion on top, for that Olde-Tyme Mexicali look.

BEEF À LA KING

4 servings

(Don't recoil from the odd-sounding combination of ingredients here, because it's actually very good. Just shut your eyes and go on opening those cans.)

All you do is mix up these things in the top of your double boiler:

1 can condensed chicken noodle soup, undiluted
1 can condensed cream of mushroom soup, undiluted
2 hard-boiled eggs, sliced
¼ pound chipped beef (you can parboil * it first to make it a little less salty, but you don't have to)
½ green pepper, chopped
3 tablespoons chopped pimento
1 teaspoon minced onion, or ½ teaspoon onion flakes

* Parboil means to boil briefly in water.

⅓ cup grated cheese or Parmesan (if you have it)
1 small can mushrooms (if you have one)

Heat it all over hot water and serve it on practically anything—toast, English muffins, rice, or in patty shells.

SKID ROAD STROGANOFF

4 *servings*

8 ounces uncooked noodles	2 teaspoons salt
1 beef bouillon cube	½ teaspoon paprika
1 garlic clove, minced	2 3-ounce cans mushrooms
⅓ cup onion, chopped	1 can condensed cream of
2 tablespoons cooking oil	chicken soup, undiluted
1 pound ground beef	1 cup commercial sour cream
2 tablespoons flour	chopped parsley

Start cooking those noodles, first dropping a bouillon cube
into the noodle water. Brown the garlic, onion, and crumbled
beef in the oil. Add the flour, salt, paprika, and mushrooms, stir, and let it cook five minutes while you light a
cigarette and stare sullenly at the sink. Then add the soup
and simmer it—in other words, cook on low flame under
boiling point—ten minutes. Now stir in the sour cream—
keeping the heat low, so it won't curdle—and let it all heat
through. To serve it, pile the noodles on a platter, pile the
Stroganoff mix on top of the noodles, and sprinkle chopped
parsley around with a lavish hand.

Now, you noticed that chopped parsley in the Stroganoff
we just passed? This is very important. You will notice a
certain dependence, in this book, on PARSLEY (which you
buy a bunch of, wash, shake, and stuff wet into a covered
Mason jar, and store in the refrigerator, where it will keep
nicely practically forever), and PARMESAN (which, if you were
a purist, you'd buy a rocklike chunk of, and grate as you
need it. Inasmuch as you're not, you buy it in bulk at an
Italian delicatessen or in a box with holes in the top, at
the grocer's), and PAPRIKA (which you buy an ordinary spice
box of and keep handy on the kitchen stove).
The reason for these little garnishes is that even though
you hate to cook, you don't always want this fact to show,
as it so often does with a plateful of nude food. So you
put light things on dark things (like Parmesan on spinach)
and dark things on light things (like parsley on sole) and
sprinkle paprika on practically everything within reach. Some-

times you end up with a dinner in which everything seems to be sprinkled with something, which gives a certain earnest look to the whole performance, but it still shows you're trying.

To repeat, the important thing is contrast. Once I knew a little girl who often made herself Cracker Sandwiches. That's right; she'd put a nice filling of oyster crackers between two slices of white bread. I think she grew up to be a hospital dietitian.

SWISS LOAF

6-7 *servings*

(*This is a somewhat more interesting sort of a meat loaf.*)

2 pounds hamburger
1½ cups diced Swiss cheese
2 beaten eggs
½ cup chopped onion
½ cup chopped green pepper
1½ teaspoons salt
½ teaspoon pepper
1 teaspoon celery salt
½ teaspoon paprika
2½ cups milk
1 cup dry bread crumbs

Just mix these things together in the approximate order they're given, then press it all into one big greased loaf pan, or use two. Bake, uncovered, at 350° for about an hour and a half, then yodel for the family.

CHILLY-NIGHT CHILI

6-8 *servings*

(*A good cheap classic chili recipe that's easy to remember because it's one of everything.*)

1 pound hamburger
1 big onion, chopped
1 or 2 cans of kidney beans, depending on how many you're feeding
1 can tomato soup, undiluted
1 teaspoon salt
1 tablespoon chili powder (then taste and add more if you like)
ripe olives, if they're handy

Brown the meat and the onion in a little butter and cook till the meat is brown—about ten minutes. Add everything else, then let it simmer covered for half an hour.

Just a word here about what to serve *with* things. You may have noticed that many recipe books are full of suggestions. "With this," they'll say, "serve Curried Peaches, crisp hot cornsticks, and Angel Torte."

The reason they do this isn't just to be helpful. Between you and me, it is also to make that entree recipe sound better. You can make meat loaf sound almost exciting, if you talk long enough about Crusty Cheese Potatoes and Heart of Artichoke Salad and Lime Sherbet and Fudge Cake, but you still haven't changed the basically pedestrian quality of the meat loaf. Furthermore, when you hate to cook, what you serve with something is what you happen to have around; and you wouldn't dream of cooking all those things for one meal anyway.

So this recipe book won't suggest accompanying dishes very often, except in cases where it is really hard to think of one, or when the entree looks a bit pathetic and needs bolstering.

Now for the LAMB department. Lamb, when you hate to cook, usually consists of chops or a leg of. It was a great day for me when I discovered lamb shanks.

LOVELY LAMB SHANKS

4-5 servings

4 lamb shanks, cracked *
1 peeled cut garlic clove
4 tablespoons flour
3 teaspoons paprika
1½ teaspoons salt
½ teaspoon pepper
3 tablespoons fat
3 cups hot water
1¼ cups raw rice

Shake your shanks, well rubbed with garlic, in a paper bag containing the flour and seasonings. Brown them on each and every side in the hot fat. Add the water and the garlic clove—speared with a toothpick, so you can find it later —and simmer covered for an hour. Then add the rice, simmer, covered, for another half hour, and you're done.

LAMB SHANKS TRA-LA

4-5 servings

(This has the easiest barbecue sauce you'll ever make, and it's very good, too.)

1 large onion, sliced thin
1 cup tomato catsup
1 cup water
½ cup mint jelly
2 tablespoons lemon juice
4 lamb shanks, cracked *
flour, salt, pepper, to dredge meat in
3 tablespoons fat

* Make sure the butcher cracks them. Otherwise, though they'll still taste good, they'll look rather like rolled-up pants legs and be harder to eat.

Combine the first five ingredients and heat them until the jelly melts. Dredge the shanks in the flour, et cetera, and brown them in the fat in a Dutch oven or electric skillet. Be sure you pour off the excess fat after they've browned. Then pour the sauce on, cover, and simmer—basting once in a while, if you happen to think of it—for an hour and a half.

LAMB CHOPS MIGNON

You start with inch-thick lamb chops. Cut the bones out of them, then wrap a bacon strip around each and fasten it with a toothpick. Put a teaspoon each of Worcestershire sauce and catsup on each chop, set them on a rack in the oven—with a drip pan beneath—and bake at 350° for about thirty-five minutes, until the bacon is crisp.

This makes a pretty company platter, incidentally, with some fat tomato slices and parsley around the edge.

OLD FAITHFUL

4 servings

(Fruit salad is good with this, because there are enough vegetables in it anyhow.)

4 medium-thick lamb or pork chops	1 tiny pinch of thyme
	1 large onion
6 tablespoons raw rice	2 ripe tomatoes
1 can consommé or broth or bouillon (chicken is best)	½ green pepper, cut in rings
	salt, pepper
1 tiny pinch of marjoram	2 tablespoons of fat

Brown the chops in the fat in a skillet. While they're browning, put the rice in the bottom of a greased casserole dish, and slice the vegetables. Next, lay the chops on the rice and top each one with slices of onion, tomato, and green pepper, salting and peppering a bit as you go. Pour the consommé in, add the marjoram and thyme, cover, and let it fend for itself in a 350° oven for an hour.

The Problem of Falling in Love You often do, when you hate to cook, fall in love with one recipe which seems to have simply everything: it's fast, it's simple, and the whole family *likes* it. And so, like impetuous lovers since time began, you tend to overdo it. You find yourself serving the little gem three times a week, including Sunday breakfast. Your problems are solved. You're serene. Oh, you love that little recipe!

But no recipe can stand such an onslaught. After a while, it just doesn't taste as good as it did the first time. You begin to wonder what you ever saw in it. Presently, you stop making it. Eventually, it's lost in limbo, and that's the end of *that* love affair.

Two things are responsible for this all-too-common occurrence: first, you overdid it, and, second, you probably started to kick it around. You felt so safe with your own true love that you began taking it for granted, not exactly following the recipe, using vinegar instead of lemon juice, or canned mushrooms instead of fresh mushrooms (because you *had* some vinegar or canned mushrooms). Soon, without your being aware of it, the recipe has undergone a sea change, and become something rich and undoubtedly strange, all right, but not at all the same recipe you started with.

The moral is this: Instead of going steady, play the field. When you make proper contact with a recipe, *don't make it again for an entire month.* Keep it warm and cozy, your ace in the hole, in your card file, or checked in your recipe book, while you try some more. Presently, you'll have several aces in the hole, which is a very delectable state of affairs indeed.

In the PORK and HAM department, we come to:

MAXIE'S FRANKS

4-6 *servings*

(*This is a fast, good franks and kraut routine.*)

½ onion, chopped (or 2 tablespoons minced dried onion)
2 tablespoons cooking oil
¾ cup catsup
¾ cup water
1 tablespoon brown sugar
1 teaspoon prepared mustard
No. 2½ can sauerkraut
10 or 12 frankfurters or hot dogs

You make the sauce first. Sauté the onion in the oil until it's tender, then add the catsup, water, sugar, and mustard, and bring to a boil. Now open the sauerkraut, drain it well, and put it in a big casserole. Arrange the frankfurters —slashed or split—on top, pour on the sauce, and bake, uncovered, at 350° for thirty minutes.

DR. MARTIN'S MIX

4-5 servings

(It takes about seven minutes to put this together. Dr. Martin is a busy man.)

Crumble 1 to 1½ pounds of pork sausage (hamburger will do, but pork is better) into a skillet and brown it. Pour off a little of the fat. Then add:

1 green pepper, chopped	1 cup raw rice
2 green onions, (also called scallions) chopped	1 tablespoon Worcestershire sauce
2 or 3 celery stalks, chopped	½ teaspoon salt
2 cups chicken consommé or bouillon	

Dr. Martin then puts the lid on and lets it simmer at the lowest possible heat while he goes out and sets a fracture. When he comes back in about an hour, his dinner is ready.

PORK CHOPS AND SPUDS

Use the grater with the big holes to grate your potatoes for scalloping; it's much faster than slicing. Then prepare them in your habitual scallop fashion, whatever that may be. (If you don't have a habitual fashion, you might put over them a can of condensed cream of mushroom soup slightly diluted with a third of a can of milk.) Lay the pork chops on top of the potatoes and put the casserole dish in a 350° oven, uncovered. If you happen to think of it, turn the chops over in half an hour and salt and pepper them. You bake this for an hour all told.

And so to CHICKEN.

It's a funny thing about chicken. Grandma got along nicely frying hers, and she lived to a sprightly old age. But these days the word is "baked," not fried—oven-baked.

That is what these two recipes are, by pure happenstance, although in the first one you cheat a bit and brown the bird first.

CHICKEN-RICE ROGER

5-6 servings

2½-pound fryer (or 2 packages frozen breasts or thighs, thawed)	1 tablespoon grated onion (or half a garlic clove, minced)
¾ cup uncooked rice	2 chicken-bouillon cubes dissolved in 1¾ cups water (or

salt, pepper
3-ounce can of mushrooms
½ stick butter

2 teaspoons instant chicken
  bouillon ditto)

Flour and then brown the chicken in a little oil. While it browns, put the rice, salt, and pepper in a greased casserole and strew the grated onion about. Put in the mushrooms, juice and all. Arrange the chicken artfully on top, pour the bouillon over it, and dot with the butter. Cover it. Bake it at 350° for an hour.

SATURDAY CHICKEN

4-6 servings

(Closely related to Sunday Chicken, p. 70.)

1 disjointed fryer (or any 6 good-sized pieces of chicken)
1 can condensed cream of mushroom soup
1 cup cream (don't cheat and use milk; the cream makes a
   lot of difference)
salt and garlic salt
paprika
chopped parsley

Take your chicken and salt and garlic salt it a bit, then paprika it thoroughly. Next, spread it out, in one layer, in a shallow baking pan. Dilute the soup with the cream, pour it over the chicken, and sprinkle the chopped parsley prettily on top. Bake it, uncovered, at 350° for one and a half hours.

Speaking of cooking, incidentally, and I believe we were, one of its worst facets is grocery shopping. When you hate to cook, a supermarket is an appalling place. You see so many things that they all blur, and you finally end up with a glazed look and a chop. So take this cookbook along when you go shopping. Then, when you see a can of shrimp, for instance, it might ring a far-away bell, and you can look in your little book to see what we'd do with it, we women who hate to cook. We'd commit

HURRY CURRY

4-6 servings

½ teaspoon curry powder
½ cup chopped onion
1 tablespoon butter

1 cup sour cream
1 cup cooked shrimp (or one
   7-ounce can)

1 can frozen condensed cream   1 cup raw rice
  of shrimp soup

Start the rice cooking. Then, in the top part of your double boiler, simmer the onion and curry powder in the butter till the onion's tender but not brown. Add the frozen soup, set the pan over hot water, and stir till it's smooth. Add the sour cream and the shrimp, and heat till it's hot clear through. Serve over hot rice, with sprigs of parsley and a spatter of paprika.

(If you keep a jar of chutney in the refrigerator—it keeps practically forever—you can serve it forth whenever you make a curry dish, and you'll feel less guilty about skipping the chopped peanuts and green onions and all those other messy little odds and ends.)

Also, even simpler and cheaper, we'd make

PORTLAND PILAFF

3-4 servings

7-ounce can shrimp
1 cup raw rice
½ stick butter (4 tablespoons)
a bit of chopped onion, green
  or otherwise

1 can chicken consommé diluted with ½ can water (or 2 chicken-bouillon cubes dissolved in 2 cups hot water)

Use a heavy ovenproof skillet. Cook the rice in the butter till it's the color of a nice camel's-hair coat. Add the consommé and onion, cover the skillet, and bake for thirty-five minutes at 325°. Now open the can of shrimp, drain them, and pour the little rascals in. (If you can afford two cans, so much the better.) Bake for ten more minutes.

CANCAN CASSEROLE

3-4 servings

(*This is about the easiest tuna casserole that ever happened, and it's quite good.*)

Beat two eggs and add a can of evaporated milk. Then add:
    No. 2 can cream-style corn
    7-ounce can chunk tuna, broken a bit with a fork
    1 green pepper, chopped
    1 middle-sized onion, grated

Pour it all into a buttered casserole dish and bake it, uncovered, at 325° for one hour.

TUNA-RICE CURRY

(*Handy to know about, because you probably have on hand everything it calls for. Incidentally, if you keep canned cream sauce in the house, it hurries things up.*)

2 teaspoons curry powder	1 can chunk tuna
2 cups cream sauce	1 onion, chopped
1 cup cooked rice (about ⅓ cup raw)	1 tablespoon parsley
	½ teaspoon salt
3 hard-boiled eggs, chopped	2 tablespoons chopped green onion (for garnish)

Mix the tuna with eggs, cooked rice, onion, parsley, and salt. Stir the curry powder into the cream sauce, add it to the tuna mixture, and bake it all in a greased casserole at 325° for an hour. Put the chopped green onions on top of it before you serve it, and put a bowl of chutney on the table.

(It is good psychology when serving a casserole dish to use individual casseroles instead of one large one. They look more interesting, and, also, if they're not entirely eaten, you need have no compunction about throwing the leftovers out; see Leftover Rule, p. 32.)

CLAM WHIFFLE

3-4 servings

(*A whiffle is a soufflé that any fool can make. This is a dandy recipe for those days when you've just had your teeth pulled. It has a nice delicate flavor, too, and it doesn't call for anything you're not apt to have around, except the clams. You can even skip the green pepper.*)

12 soda crackers (the ordinary 2-inch by 2-inch kind)	1 tablespoon chopped green pepper
1 cup milk	¼ teaspoon Worcestershire sauce
¼ cup melted butter	
1 can minced clams, drained	dash of salt, pepper
2 tablespoons chopped onion	2 eggs beaten together

Soak the crumbled crackers in the milk for a few minutes. Then add everything else, eggs last, pour it all into a greased casserole, and bake it in a 350° oven for forty-five minutes, uncovered.

SOLE SURVIVOR

4 servings

(*Except for plain fried fish, this is the easiest sole recipe I've run into. You can make it with halibut, too.*)

4 sole fillets
1 can frozen shrimp soup, thawed

Heat the soup while you lay out the fish effectively in a shallow greased baking dish. Bake the fish at 400° for twenty minutes. Then reduce the heat to 300°, pour the soup over the fish, and bake it for another fifteen minutes.

CELERY FISH STICKS

4 servings

1 package frozen fish sticks, thawed
1 can condensed cream of celery soup
½ cup milk
1½ tablespoons chopped chives or green onion tops
1 tablespoon lemon juice
3 tablespoons grated Cheddar
paprika

Put the fish sticks in a shallow buttered baking dish. Thin the celery soup with the milk, and measure out a cupful. (Save the rest for somebody's lunch or throw it out.) Add the chives, lemon juice, and cheese to the thinned soup, pour it over the fish sticks, and sprinkle with paprika. Bake it at 425° for twenty minutes.

A parenthetical note here. It is understood that when you hate to cook, you buy already-prepared foods as often as you can. You buy frozen things and ready-mix things, as well as pizza from the pizza man and chicken pies from the chicken-pie lady.

But let us amend that statement. Let us say, instead, that you buy these things as often as you dare, for right here you usually run into a problem with the basic male. The average man doesn't care much for the frozen-food department, nor for the pizza man, nor for the chicken-pie lady. He wants to see you knead that bread and tote that bale, before you go down cellar to make the soap. This is known as Woman's Burden.

But sometimes you can get around it. Say, for instance, that you are serving some good dinner rolls that you bought frozen and then merely put into the oven for a few minutes, as the directions said to. At dinner, you taste them critically. Then you say, "Darn it, I simply can't make decent rolls, and that's all there is to it!"

If you are lucky, and have been able to keep him out of the kitchen while you were removing the wrapping, he will probably say, "What's the matter with you? These taste swell."

Then you say, in a finicky sort of female voice, "I don't know—they just don't seem as *light* as they ought to, or something. . . ." And the more stoutly he affirms that they're okay, the tighter the box you've got him in. Admittedly, this is underhanded, but, then, marriage is sometimes a rough game.

And don't worry one minute because it's a little more expensive to buy these things than to make them. Maybe you're hell for house cleaning. Or maybe you do your own wallpapering, while that lady down the block, who so virtuously rolls her own noddles, pays vast sums to paper hangers. Maybe you make your own clothes, or sell Christmas cards at home, or maybe you're just plain cute to have around the house.

As we slog our way through the month, let us not forget about BEANS. It is a rare budget that doesn't benefit from a modest bean dish once in a while.

Most of the time, when you hate to cook, you just add a little extra chopped onion, chili sauce, and a tablespoon of molasses to the can of beans you bought at the grocer's, and you bake them about thirty minutes at 325°, and they're very good, too.

If you feel exceptionally energetic though, you can also add a can of apple slices and a can of chopped luncheon meat to those other ingredients. This is good makeweight for growing boys, should you be blessed with any.

Also, if you have some kidney beans around, you can make

HOMEBODY BEANS

3-4 servings

(*This couldn't be better or simpler, except that you must be around to service it every two hours for six hours. Don't be afraid those already-cooked beans will cook to a pulp. For some mysterious reason, they don't.*)

2 average-size (1-pound) cans kidney beans
½ pound bacon, the leaner the better
3 big raw tomatoes (or an equal quantity of drained canned tomatoes; raw are better)
2 raw onions, sliced

In a casserole dish, alternate layers of the beans, the thick-sliced tomatoes, and the onions till you run out. Bake at 300° for two hours, uncovered.

Now cut the bacon in half (the short strips work better) and lay half of them on top. Put the casserole back in the oven, uncovered, for another two hours, by which time the bacon should be brown. Punch it down into the beans, and put the rest of your bacon strips on top. Bake it uncovered for another two hours, and you're done.

Or you can make

BURGUNDY BEANS

2 1-pound cans kidney beans	½ green pepper, chopped
3 green onions, chopped	½ pound ground beef
2 tomatoes, chopped	1 cup red wine

Just fry the onions and green pepper in a little oil until they're tender, then add the crumbled ground beef and brown it. Next, add the chopped tomatoes and the wine, and simmer it all for five minutes. Add the beans, pour it all into a casserole, and bake, uncovered, for thirty minutes in a 350° oven.

Then there is always CHEESE.

Now cheese is something of a yes-and-no proposition. It isn't too trustworthy, because you have to concentrate on it; and when you hate to cook, you don't want to. After you've produced a curdled Welsh Rabbit or a Welsh Rabbit that resembles a sullen puddle of rubber cement, the tendency is to leave cheese severely alone.

However, cheese has the virtue of keeping nicely, so long as you haven't unwrapped it (or so long as it's grated and in a covered jar in your refrigerator; see Leftover chapter). And when there's a good half-pound or so of cheese in your refrigerator, you always have a comfortable awareness that there's at least one supper on ice. (What that supper will probably be is soup and Grilled Cheese Sandwiches, and there's nothing the matter with that, either, particularly if you spread the bread with butter and a little dry mustard mixed with vinegar.)

Then there are these two recipes. Neither can make a monkey out of you, and they are both very good.

CHEESE AND WINE BAKE

4 servings

6 to 8 slices stale or lightly toasted bread	butter, garlic clove
	1 teaspoon salt
½ cup chicken bouillon	1 teaspoon Worcestershire sauce
½ pound Swiss cheese, grated (2 cups)	
	½ teaspoon mustard
1 cup dry white wine	½ teaspoon paprika
3 eggs	½ teaspoon p pper

Ready? Mince the garlic clove and cream it into enough butter to spread the bread with. Then spread it, and put the slices butter side down in a big shallow cake pan or casserole dish.

Beat up the eggs, and to them add the wine, the bouillon, all the seasonings, and the cheese. Pour this over the bread, and bake, *uncovered,* at 325° for thirty minutes.

(This is a handy dish, incidentally, if you're going out somewhere, to a cocktail party, for instance, before dinner. Before you go, you can do everything up to pouring the mixture over the bread.)

CHEESE-RICE PUDDING

4 servings

(*A cross between a pudding and a soufflé. If you like, you can serve it with mushroom sauce—some of the canned varieties aren't bad—or creamed tuna, or you can top it with a few bacon strips.*)

1 cup rice	2 tablespoons melted butter
4 eggs	¼ pound grated sharp cheese
2 cups milk	(1 cup)
	1 teaspoon salt

Cook the rice, without salt. Then separate the eggs. Beat the yolks slightly, add the milk, butter, cheese, salt, and cooked rice. Beat those egg whites now till they're very stiff. Fold them into the egg yolk-milk business. Pour it into a greased baking dish and bake at 350°, uncovered, for twenty-five minutes.

Finally, let us—all of us ladies who hate to cook—give a thought to soup.

A hearty soup, that is. A satisfying soup. A soup that —with crackers, carrot strips, and a dessert made by somebody else—will fill up the family. Here are three good ones.

HEIDELBERG SOUP

3-4 servings

2 cans frozen potato soup, diluted with
   milk according to directions on can
5 slices bacon, chopped
4 slices salami, slivered
12 green onions, chopped, including some of
   the green
black pepper
parsley

Thaw the soup in the top part of a double boiler. Meanwhile, fry the chopped bacon, drain it, and pour off all but one tablespoon of fat. In it, fry the salami and the onions. Add them, plus the bacon you just cooked, to the soup. Parsley and pepper it up, and serve.

BISQUE QUICK

6 *servings*

2 cans tomato soup, condensed
½ can pea soup, condensed
1 can chicken consommé or bouillon
1 cup thick cream
1 can crab meat, shrimp, or lobster
¾ cup sherry

Heat everything but the wine in the top of your double boiler. Just before you serve it, add the sherry.

HONEST JOHN'S CLAM CHOWDER

3 *servings*

(*As a matter of fact, this isn't exactly honest, because it doesn't call for salt pork. But who has salt pork around these days, besides butchers? The clams are canned, too, instead of fresh. But it tastes honest.*)

2 slices bacon, chopped
1 medium onion, chopped
7-ounce can minced clams
1 medium potato, shredded on large-holed grater or thin-sliced
2½ to 3 cups of milk
good sprinkling of salt and pepper

Fry the chopped bacon and onion together till the onion is tender. Add the potato, the clam juice from the can, and enough water to cover the potato. Simmer till potato is tender —ten to fifteen minutes. Add the clams, the milk, and the salt and pepper, heat, and serve it with a good big chunk of butter melting in the middle.

That's thirty. Of course, some months contain thirty-one days. But on the thirty-first, you eat out.

Chapter 2

The Leftover

or Every Family Needs a Dog

SOME WOMEN can keep a leftover going like an eight-day clock. Their Sunday's roast becomes Monday's hash, which becomes Tuesday's Stuffed Peppers, which eventually turn up as Tamale Pie, and so on, until it disappears or Daddy does. These people will even warm up stale cake and serve it with some sort of a sauce, as some sort of a pudding.

But when you hate to cook, you don't do this. You just go around thinking you ought to. So, much as you dislike that little glass jar half full of Chicken à la King, you don't throw it away, because that would be wasteful. Anyway, you read somewhere that you can put spoonfuls of it into tiny three-cornered pastry affairs and serve them hot, as hors d'oeuvres.

Actually, you know, deep down, that you never will. You also know you won't eat it yourself for lunch tomorrow because you won't feel like it, and you know it won't fit into tomorrow night's dinner, which is going to be liver and bacon, and you know you can't palm it off on Junior (kept piping hot in his little school-going thermos) because he wouldn't even touch it last night when it was new. You know how Junior is about pimentos.

But still you can't quite bring yourself to dispose of it! So you put it in the refrigerator, and there it stays, moving slowly toward the rear as it is displaced by other little glass jars half full of leftover ham loaf and other things. And there it remains until refrigerator-cleaning day, at which time you gather it up along with its little fur-bearing friends, and, with a great lightening of spirit, throw it away.

Do you know the really basic trouble here? It is your guilt complex. This is the thing you have to lick. And it isn't easy. We live in a cooking-happy age. You watch your friends redoing their kitchens and hoarding their pennies for glamorous cooking equipment and new cookbooks called *Eggplant Comes to the Party* or *Let's Waltz into the Kitchen*, and presently you begin to feel un-American.

Indeed, it is the cookbooks you already have that are to blame for your bad conscience and, hence, for your leftover problems. For instance, consider that two-thirds of a cupful of leftover creamed corn. They'll tell you to use it as a base for something they call Scrumptious Stuffed Tomatoes. Mix some bread crumbs and chopped celery with the corn and season it well, they'll say, with a fine vague wave of the hand, and then stuff this into your hollowed-out tomatoes and bake them.

Now, ideas like this are all very well for the lady who likes to cook. This is a challenge to her creative imagination. Furthermore, she'll know *how* to season it well (coriander? chervil?) and while the result may not be precisely Scrumptious, it will probably be reasonably okay.

However, if you hate to cook, you'll do better to skip the creamed-corn gambit and simply slice those nice red tomatoes into thick chunks and spread them prettily on some nice green parsley or watercress and sprinkle them with salt and papper and chopped chives and serve them forth. Because you're not about to use much creative imagination on that stuffing, inasmuch as the whole idea didn't send you very far to begin with; and your Scrumptious Stuffed Tomatoes are going to taste like tomatoes stuffed with left-over corn.

Then there is another thing these cookbooks do. They

seem to consider *everything* a leftover, which you must do something with.

For instance, cake. This is like telling you what to do with your leftover whisky. Cake isn't a leftover. Cake is cake, and it is either eaten or it isn't eaten; and if the family didn't go for that Mocha Frosting, you give the rest of the cake to the neighbor or to the lady downstairs before it gets stale. (Maybe *she'll* make something out of it, but you won't have to eat it. Maybe she'll even throw it away, but if so, you won't know about it, so it won't hurt. Like what happened to that twenty-second batch of nameless kittens you finally had to take to the city pound, there are some things you don't exactly want to know.) And certainly you don't want to let the cake get stale so you can make a Stale-Cake Pudding for the family. They're the ones who left so much of it the first time, remember?

Or cheese. Cookbooks will tell you what to do with your leftover cheese. But cheese isn't a leftover; it's a staple. If you'll grate those odd bits and put them in a covered jar in your refrigerator, *toward the front,* you may remember to sprinkle it on things, sometimes, and use it for grilled cheese sandwiches. (Don't believe what they tell you about wrapping cheese in a cloth dipped in wine to keep it fresh, because this doesn't work; it just wastes the wine. Vinegar, used the same way, is somewhat more satisfactory, but it is still an awful nuisance.)

And eggs! Most recipe books show tremendous concern about the egg white, if you didn't use the white, or the egg yolk, if you didn't use the yolk. There are four thousand things you can make and do with an egg white or an egg yolk, all of which call for more cooking and usually result in more leftovers, which is what you were trying to get away from in the first place.

The one thing they don't mention is giving the egg yolk or the egg white to the dog. It's very good for his complexion, and for cats' complexions, too. What did that egg cost? No more than a nickel, probably, and half of that is two and a half cents, which would be cheap for a beauty treatment at twice the price.

Right here we've come to the heart of the matter. Your leftovers were never very expensive to start with. Does the wild rice get left over? Or the choice red out-of-season strawberries? No. It's that dreary little mess of mixed vegetables, worth about six mills in a bull market. You have to think these things through.

Just one more word about the leftover before we get down to where the work is. Home Ec-sperts and other people who made straight A's in Advanced Cream Sauce have gone so far as to rename leftovers "Plan-overs." They actually want you to cook up a lot more of something than you'll need, and then keep it around to ring exciting changes on, as they put it, through the weeks to come.

It's true that certain people like certain things better the next day. Scalloped potatoes, when they're fried in butter. Or potato salad. Or baked beans. Every family has its little ways. And it's perfectly true that leftover Spanish Rice or Tamale Loaf makes an adequate stuffing for Baked Stuffed Green Peppers, if you get around to doing it before the Spanish Rice or Tamale Loaf starts looking disconsolate.

But when you hate to cook, don't ever fall into the Plan-over Trap. You'll end up hating yourself, too, as you think of that great pile of Something which you'll have to plow through before you can once again face the world clear-eyed and empty-handed.

The word is this: Pare the recipe, if you need to, so that there is only enough for the meal you're faced with. Then buy, as the French do, in small niggling quantities. What is a lady profited if she gains two avocados for nineteen cents instead of one for a dime if she doesn't need the second one and so lets it blacken away?

And the motto to paint on your refrigerator door is this:

WHEN IN DOUBT, THROW IT OUT.

Just remember: if vegetables have been cooked twice, there aren't enough vitamins left in them to dust a fiddle with. Furthermore, if your refrigerator is jam-packed with little jars, it will have to work too hard to keep things cold. Presently its arteries will harden, and you will have to pay for a service call—the price of which would more than buy a lovely dinner out for you and your husband, with red-coated servitors and soft music.

Finally, and possibly most important, all those leftovers are hard on the family's morale when they open the refrigerator door. Wondering what's for dinner, they begin to get a pretty grim idea, and presently they begin to wonder what's with Mother. The inside of her icebox doesn't look like the insides of the iceboxes they see in the magazine pictures, and Mother loses face.

Actually, the only sort of leftover you need to concern yourself with is meat. It takes more character than most of us have—even those of us who hate to cook—to throw out two or three pounds of cooked beef, lamb, ham, pork, or turkey. So let us consider the meat problem.

Before you do a thing with that great sullen chunk of protein, ask yourself a few questions:

Have you incorporated it into a dish of scalloped potatoes, with plenty of cheese on top?

Have you augmented it with a few slices of Swiss cheese from the delicatessen and served it forth as a Toasted Club Sandwich, in neat triangles surrounding a mound of coleslaw or fruit salad?

Have you re-presented it as an honest cold-cut platter, with deviled eggs in the middle, and ready-mix corn muffins on the side? It's easy to forget the obvious.

And have you ground up a chunk of it with pickles and onions and celery and added some mayonnaise, as a spread for after-school sandwiches?

If you can truthfully answer yes to the foregoing, then, as the British say, you are for it. You are about to start cooking.

This is a good recipe you can make out of *any* leftover meat.

LET 'ER BUCK

4 servings

1 loaf French bread, cut in half lengthwise
1 jar mild-flavored processed cheese spread
sliced or chopped leftover meat (fried crumbled hamburger works fine, too)

2 small cans mushrooms
1½ teaspoons oregano
¾ cup chopped green onion
1½ cans tomato sauce
4 tablespoons olive oil (or other salad oil)

Spread a big piece of aluminum foil, cupping the edges so the juice won't run over, on a cookie sheet or in a shallow baking pan. Place the two halves of bread on it, cut side up. Then, working coolly and efficiently, spread the next five ingredients, in the order listed, on the bread. Be sure you spread the cheese clear to the edge, all over, because this keeps the bread from getting soggy. Then spoon the tomato sauce on top and, finally, drizzle the oil over the works. Don't broil it—just put it in a 325° oven for twenty minutes.

And here are some things besides hash, stuffed peppers, and shepherd's pie that you can make out of LEFTOVER ROAST BEEF.

BEEF YORKSHIRE

4-5 servings

(This is Yorkshire pudding for cowards. It assumes that you saved five or six tablespoons of beef drippings. If you didn't, you might keep it in mind for next time.)

First, start the sauce, so it will be ready when the Beef Yorkshire is.

Sauce Brown 1½ tablespoons of flour in 1½ tablespoons of butter, in a saucepan over low heat. Slowly add a can of beef consommé, and stir till it's smooth and a bit thick. Let it simmer half an hour, add a dash of Worcestershire, and keep it hot in the double boiler.

Now you need:

5 to 6 tablespoons beef drippings
6 medium-thick slices of leftover beef
1 package popover mix (plus the eggs and milk it calls for)

Set your oven for 400°. Put the beef drippings in a 9 x 13-inch cake pan and melt them. Lay the beef slices on top of the drippings. Mix the popover mix as the package tells you to, and pour it evenly over the beef slices. When your oven has reached 400°, and it certainly should have by this time, put the pan in and bake it for forty minutes. Serve with the hot sauce.

HUSHKABOBS

(So-called because the family isn't supposed to know it's just that old Sunday roast still following them around.)

You need a barbecue skewer per person.
You also need:

> inch-size beef cubes, 5 per person
> large mushroom caps, canned or
>   otherwise (or green pepper strips)
> canned small whole onions
> quartered greenish tomatoes

First you make a marinade by mixing

¼ cup cheap red wine   1 cut garlic clove
¼ cup olive oil   pinch of thyme and oregano

Let the beef cubes sit in this for three or four hours, and stir them occasionally. Then string them on skewers, alternating with the vegetables, which you also brush with the marinade before cooking.

If it's barbecue season, barbecue them. If not, the stove broiler works fine (but be sure you place a pan underneath the skewers or you'll have a mess on the oven floor).

In either case, cook them fast, close to the heat. You cooked that meat once, you know. All it has to do now is brown.

BEEF ENCORE
(Known in some circles as Eiffel Trifle.)

leftover roast beef, sliced thin   1 tablespoon flour
1 cut garlic clove   ½ teaspoon paprika
2 onions, thinly sliced   ½ cup white wine
1 tablespoon butter   1 cup beef consommé
                                    1 teaspoon good wine vinegar

First, melt the butter in a skillet, then sizzle the cut garlic clove in it for two minutes and remove it *immediately*. Put the onions where the garlic used to be, and sprinkle the flour over them. Stir until it is light brown, add the wine and consommé and cook very slowly for fifteen minutes. Add the meat and paprika. Don't let the sauce boil now. Simmer just long enough to heat the meat through—about five minutes. Just before you serve it, add the wine vinegar.

And here are three things to do with LEFTOVER ROAST LAMB.

GOOD LEFTOVER LAMB SANDWICHES
(With soup, there's supper.)

Grind up about two cups of your leftover lamb and add three tablespoons of grated Parmesan cheese. Add more mayonnaise to make a good smooth spread, and add some prepared mustard and horse-radish, too, according to your taste. Then spread it on thin-sliced buttered dark bread—pumpernickel or rye—with lettuce.

INDONESIAN CURRY

6 servings

(This is a mild curry which came from Indonesia via San Francisco, with a short but pleasant stopover in Grants Pass.)

5 tablespoons butter	1 cup water
1 cup chopped onion	2 cups diced leftover lamb
2 apples, peeled and chopped	4 tablespoons flour
2 cans beef consommé	2 teaspoons curry powder
juice of 1 lemon	1½ cups raw rice

Sauté the onion and the apple together in a deep skillet until they're tender, using two tablespoons of the butter. Then add the rest of the butter, and sift the flour and curry powder in, too. Stir all this until it's comfortably integrated. Then add the consommé and the water, lemon juice, and cubed lamb. Simmer it all from half an hour to an hour, while the rice cooks.

This gives you a nice little breather. You may now put your feet up and have a highball, or else you may dirty up a lot of little dishes with

chopped peanuts	sliced bananas
chopped green onions	grated orange rind
chopped almonds	crumbled bacon
toasted coconut	raisins
diced cucumber	chutney

to serve as side boys with your curry. Take your choice.

LAMB PEPPERS

6 servings

(*You can use leftover veal for this, too.*)

Cut the stem ends off six pretty green peppers and take the seeds out, then parboil the peppers five minutes, or till they're barely tender. Now mix together:

¾ cup finely chopped lamb	½ cup finely chopped tomato
½ cup bread crumbs	½ teaspoon salt
½ cup chicken consommé or bouillon	½ teaspoon garlic salt
	1 teaspoon vinegar

Stuff this into the peppers and bake them in a 350° oven for fifteen minutes, in a greased pan.

Now let us assume you're about to grapple with a HAM, or what's left of one. Nothing looks bigger. On the other hand, there are many things you can do with it—ham loaf, ham croquettes, ham-and-egg pie, et cetera—recipes for which you can find in your big fat cookbook. Here are three you probably can't.

HAM-LIMA SUPPER

6 servings

2 cups diced ham
2 No. 2 cans lima beans
¼ cup olive oil
4 whole green onions, sliced
1 teaspoon salt
½ teaspoon sugar
dash of cayenne
½ green pepper, chopped
3 good-sized tomatoes, sliced
¼ cup grated Parmesan

First cook the onions in the oil till they're light brown. Add the green pepper, cayenne, sugar, salt, and the drained beans (and throw the juice out). Toss all this for three or four minutes in the pan. Then spread all the diced ham in the bottom of an ungreased casserole, cover it with the bean mixture, spread the sliced tomatoes on top of *that,* and sprinkle the Parmesan on top of everything. Bake it, uncovered, for thirty minutes at 350°.

JUDY O'GRADY'S HAM

6 servings

First, cook two cups of noodles till they're tender. Next, grind up

½ pound leftover ham
½ pound sharp Cheddar
1 teaspoon horse-radish

Then add to it

½ teaspoon salt
1 green pepper
1 can condensed cream of mushroom, chicken, or celery soup thinned with ¼ cup milk

Whistling cheerily, you may now mix everything together, including the noodles, and bake it, covered, in a buttered casserole at 350° for forty minutes. Then remove the cover, sprinkle some crumbs on top, dot with butter, and brown it under the broiler.

THE COLONEL'S LADY'S HAM

5-6 servings

½ pound ham, cut in strips
2 tablespoons butter
½ cup chopped onion
2 teaspoons flour
1 cup sour cream
6-ounce can mushrooms
1¼ cups rice

Start cooking the rice to serve it on. Then sauté the ham strips and onion in the butter till the onion is tender. Sprinkle the flour over it, stir it in, make sure the heat's low, then gradually stir in the sour cream and the mushrooms.

Stir this conscientiously for a few minutes while it all thickens, and that's it.

Then there is always LEFTOVER PORK.

Remember, it's very nice sliced cold, served with cold applesauce.

You can also make

GUNG HO

(*This is so simple it's embarrassing; but everyone likes it, including little children, which is a big point.*)

You cut the leftover pork in strips, removing as much fat as you can. If you saved some of the good brown pan drippings, add a little water—say a third of a cup—stir it up and heat, then add enough chicken consommé or bouillon to make a reasonable amount of sauce. (If you didn't save any drippings, the consommé alone is all right.) You now add the pork strips to this and heat them in it, then pour it all over cooked, hot, drained Chinese noodles. Top with chopped green onions and pass the soy sauce.

SUB GUM YUK

3-4 *servings*

First you take a can of chow mein noodles and put three quarters of it in a bowl. Set the rest aside for topping later. Now mix up with the noodles you put in the bowl

1 can condensed cream of mushroom soup	¼ cup chopped onion
	½ teaspoon salt, pepper
¼ cup water	2 teaspoons soy sauce or sherry
1 cup diced leftover pork	
1 cup sliced celery	¼ cup chopped cashews or walnuts

Put this into a buttered casserole dish, top with the rest of the noodles, and if you have any more nuts around, in addition to that quarter-cupful, put them on top of the noodles. Bake, uncovered, at 350° for thirty minutes. (This is very good, incidentally, made with a 7-ounce can of chunk tuna instead of the leftover pork.)

LEFTOVER CHICKEN: Who ever has any leftover chicken? I never have any to speak of, and neither does anyone else I know—just a leftover drumstick once in a while, and what you do with that is eat it.

LEFTOVER TURKEY is, of course, a bird of a different

feather. The following two recipes are good because they don't make the starry-eyed assumption that you have a lot of gravy and dressing left over.

TURKEY DIVAN

5-6 servings

6 good-sized slices of turkey
1 can condensed cream of chicken soup
   (thinned slightly with 2 tablespoons sherry
   and a little cream)
1 package frozen broccoli, cooked
grated Parmesan cheese

Put about one fourth of the soup mixture in a buttered casserole. Put the broccoli in, cover it with slices of turkey meat, and pour on the rest of the sauce. Sprinkle the Parmesan generously on top and bake at 350°, uncovered, for about twenty minutes.

TURKEY TETRAZZINI

5-6 servings

(*This isn't exactly a lead-pipe cinch, because you have to make that cream sauce; but if you ever have to have company the day after Thanksgiving, you'll thank me for it.*)

½ pound spaghetti
¼ pound fresh mushrooms
5 tablespoons butter
⅓ cup flour
2 cups turkey broth or chicken consommé
1 cup light cream
2 tablespoons sherry
2 cups diced turkey
½ cup grated Parmesan
salt, pepper

First, you cook the spaghetti the way the package tells you to. Now slice the mushrooms and sauté them in a tablespoon of the butter till they're light brown.

Then you make the cream sauce: Blend four tablespoons of butter with the flour in the top of a double boiler, add the turkey broth, and cook it, stirring, till it's smooth and thick. Add the cream, salt, pepper, and sherry.

Now divide the sauce in half. In one half put the turkey meat, and in the other half put the mushrooms and cooked spaghetti. (At this point you may wonder why you ever started this, but actually you're nearly out of the woods.)

Put the spaghetti-mushroom half in a greased casserole and make a hole in it. Into the hole pour the turkey half. Top it with the Parmesan, and bake, uncovered, at 400° for twenty minutes.

And next time, for heaven's sake, get a *little* turkey!

Chapter 3

Vegetables, Salads, Salad Dressings
or This Side of Beriberi

ONCE I knew a girl who just loved vegetables. You didn't dare leave this little bunny alone with a relish tray or it would be instantly deflowered of its cauliflowerlets and stripped clean of its carrot strips.

But this girl is in the minority. For cold scientific proof, do this: On one side of a plate, put a stack of marinated string beans; on the other side, put a heap of smoked oysters. Then observe carefully which gets left. You needn't even be that fancy. A can of salted peanuts will win over the string beans, hands down, every time.

Facts must be faced. Vegetables simply don't taste as good as most other things do. And there isn't a single vegetable, hot or cold, that stands on its own two feet the way a ripe peach does, or a strawberry. Even sweet corn needs butter and salt. (It is interesting to note that vegetables beginning with A are the most self-sufficient: artichokes, asparagus, avocados, which have really slithered out of the fruit kingdom by this time into the vegetable kingdom, no matter what the botanists say. But the farther down the alphabet you go, through rutabagas, spinach, and turnips, the more hopeless they become, given all the butter and salt you've got.)

Actually, the food experts know this, too, 'way down deep. You can tell they do, from the reliance they put on adjectives whenever they bump into a vegetable. "And with it serve a big bowl of tiny, buttery, fresh-from-the-garden beets!" they'll cry. But they're still only beets, and there's no need to get so excited about it.

Never make the mistake of combining two rather repulsive vegetables in the hope that any good will come of it. *Two wrongs never make a right.* Once I knew a lady who cooked big carrots and hollowed out their middles and filled the resultant canoes with canned peas.

In order to make most vegetables fit to eat, you must cover up the basic taste of the vitamins with calories. You use butter, oil, sour cream, nuts, chopped bacon, mushrooms, and cheese, as well as lemon juice, vinegar, herbs, and a lot of other things which we shall come to presently.

This is not only fattening, for the most part, but it is also a lot of trouble. You're certainly not going to do it very often. There is no reason you should, either. The children must learn sooner or later that life isn't all beer and skittles, and your husband knows it anyhow. It won't hurt them a bit to eat their plain buttered vegetables at gun point, with a running commentary by you on what will happen to their teeth and complexions and bottoms if they don't.

Moreover, there is a certain social cachet to serving your vegetables plain. Indeed, if your entree is in any way fancy, the *haute cuisine* crowd frowns on anything but the simplest vegetable as an accompaniment, which should be a load off your mind and off your back.

So just gird your loins and serve that big bowl of tiny, buttery, fresh-from-the-garden beets, murmuring—if you care to—"After all, there's nothing like good butter, salt, and coarse-ground pepper." (Always be sure it's coarse-ground, because a lot of people feel that anything peppered should look as though it had been fished out of a gravel pit.)

However, just once in a while, when you are serving a

very easy main dish, like something thawed, or when you yourself get so tired of plain vegetables that you cannot stand them any more, it is nice to know a few things to do.

First of all, find a commercial seasoning you like, and add it to the melted butter. This is an easy way to improve vast hordes of vegetables.

Second, you can also add a bouillon cube, or a teaspoon of instant bouillon, to the water you cook them in. This helps a bit, too.

Third, the authorities maintain that a wee pinch of sugar, in addition to your other seasonings, brings out the flavor of *any* vegetable. The debatable point here is whether you want to bring it out or cover it up; but this is every girl's own personal decision.

Fourth, there is an easy cheese sauce you can make and keep on hand to give a gentle assist to cauliflower, cabbage, asparagus, green beans, et cetera.

EASY CHEESE SAUCE

1 pound sharp processed cheese, diced
1½ cups evaporated milk
1½ teaspoons salt
2 teaspoons dry mustard

Melt the cheese in the top of your double boiler over hot water, add everything else, and stir it till it's smooth and hot. Then pour it into a jar, cover it, and keep it in the refrigerator. When you want to use some of it, put the amount you want in the top of your double boiler again, thin it with a little milk, and heat it.

Fifth, there is an easy fake hollandaise which is good with artichokes, asparagus, and whatever else you think you'd like hollandaise on.

FAKE HOLLANDAISE

¾ cup mayonnaise   salt, pepper
⅓ cup milk   1 teaspoon lemon juice

Cook the milk and mayonnaise together in the top of your double boiler for five minutes, stirring constantly. Then add the other things and stir just long enough for one good chorus of "Gloomy Sunday," and it's done.

And so to the recipes.

COMPANY CARROTS

3-4 servings

(Through the ages, people have gone to enormous trouble to camouflage carrots. Once I saw a recipe that called for carrots, strained honey, oregano, grated Swiss cheese, and chestnuts, which is like sewing diamond buttons on denim pants.)

Cut a reasonable number of carrots into strips—so you have two cupfuls, say. Cook them till they're tender and drain them. Then mix these things together in a skillet:

3 tablespoons butter	½ teaspoon paprika
2 tablespoons sugar	juice of half a lemon

Add the carrots and sauté them about ten minutes, stirring so that all the strips get well acquainted with the sauce.

OVEN CARROTS

4-5 servings

(If you're out of lemon juice and feel that you must do something about carrots anyway, you can do this. It is more trouble, but it demands no last-minute attention, the carrots stay crisp, and the dish looks quite polite.)

4 green onions chopped, tops and all	3 tablespoons minced parsley
3 tablespoons butter	1 teaspoon salt
10 to 12 small carrots, or 5 big ones, cut in strips	dash of pepper
	¼ cup light cream

Fry the onions in the butter till they're tender. Add the carrots, parsley, salt, and pepper, and put it all into a buttered casserole dish. Pour the cream on top, cover, and bake at 350° for forty-five minutes.

KIDS VS. CARROTS

Children who raise Cain about carrots will sometimes eat them if you boil them along with potatoes and mash the two together. Not always, but sometimes.

VERY EDIBLE STRING BEANS

6 servings

(Many string bean recipes, too, call for expensive ingredients like fresh mushrooms and toasted almonds, and even so, you can still taste the string beans. Simmering them with a ham

bone works as well as anything, but remember, they didn't give that ham bone away. This recipe calls for no exotic extras, and it tastes good.)

2 packages frozen string
  beans, cooked and
  drained (or 2 pounds fresh
  ditto)
5 tablespoons butter

salt and pepper
1 tablespoon finely chopped
  parsley
1 clove garlic, minced
juice of half a lemon

Sauté the cooked beans in the butter, along with the salt, pepper, parsley, and garlic, for seven to ten minutes. Just before you serve them, sprinkle the lemon juice on. (Note: These beans are the exception that proves the Leftover Rule, p. 32. If there are any beans left over, known as has-beans, you had better keep them, because they are good in a green salad.)

BEN'S BEANS

All he does is this: He sautés a little can or two of mushroom pieces in a little butter, adds cooked green beans, salt, pepper. Then, over low heat, he stirs in enough sour cream to make a sauce, heats it through, and serves it up.

If you are roasting meat in a 300° oven and want a vegetable to bake along with it, you can make

SIMPLE BEANS

3-4 servings

Cook and drain a package of frozen string beans and add

1 tablespoon minced onion
½ teaspoon salt
¾ cup condensed mushroom soup thinned
  a bit with rich milk
2 tablespoons chopped pimentos if you have them

Put this in a casserole dish and bake it, uncovered, for an hour in that 300° oven. Longer won't hurt. (Canned string beans work fine in this recipe, too.)

BEETNIKS

Should you happen to fish the final sweet pickle out of the juice in a pickle jar and, at the same instant, notice a can of shoestring or baby beets on the pantry shelf (admittedly an unlikely chain of events), you can put the beets into the pickle juice, put the lid back on, and the next morning they will be pickled.

SOUR CREAM CABBAGE

5-6 servings

(You wouldn't cook this for company unless your kitchen is two blocks from the living room, but it's easy and it tastes good.)

1 firm green cabbage	½ teaspoon nutmeg
1 egg, well beaten	salt and pepper
2 tablespoons sugar	1 cup sour cream

Shred the cabbage fine, and throw the core away. Cook it in as little water as possible till it's tender—five to ten minutes. Drain it, then add the other ingredients, mixed together, and put it on a low burner to heat through.

THE SOLUTION TO CANNED PEAS

4 servings

First, buy a pound can of little tiny ones. Drain them. Then slice three green onions and sizzle them a minute in one tablespoon of olive oil. Add the peas, and

¼ teaspoon thyme	¼ head lettuce, chopped
dash of salt, pepper	

and stir it once in a while as it sits on a low burner and heats through.

BROILED ONIONS

4 servings

1 pound can small cooked onions	¼ cup bread crumbs
	¼ cup grated Parmesan
2 tablespoons butter	salt, pepper

You drain the onions first, then rinse them with cold water. Melt the butter in a pie tin and roll the onions in it. Now mix the bread crumbs and Parmesan together and sprinkle the mixture all over the little fellows, before setting them four inches beneath a hot broiler for seven minutes.

IDIOT ONIONS

3 servings

Combine a can of drained small onions with a can of cream sauce (or make two cups of your own and add a dash of Worcestershire to it). Put the mixture in a flat pan, sprinkle Parmesan heavily on top, and bake at 325° for twenty-five minutes.

CRISP TOMATOES

Cut some firm tomatoes into thick slices, salt and pepper them, dip them in cornmeal, and pan fry them in bacon fat or butter until they're light brown.

PAINLESS SPINACH

4 *servings*

1 package frozen spinach   salt
1 cut garlic clove   pepper
1 tablespoon butter   half a lemon

First, cook the spinach and drain it. Then sizzle the garlic clove in the butter, remove the clove, and put the spinach in. Let it simmer for five minutes. Just before you serve it, salt and pepper it lightly and add a good squeeze of lemon juice.

SPINACH SURPRISE

4 *servings*

(*The surprise is that there's usually none left, even with dedicated antispinach people.*)

1 package frozen chopped   4 tablespoons butter
   spinach   pinch of salt
¼ cup chopped onion   ½ cup sour cream
                              1 teaspoon vinegar

Cook the spinach with the onion. Melt the butter, add the spinach, well drained, and stir it about. Then add the salt and sour cream, and blend it together. Finally, stir in the vinegar and serve.

And so to the SALAD department.

Many dishes have been called salad, including canned peach slices in lime Jello, bananas, walnuts and whipped cream, and cottage cheese. Once, I knew a lady who pitted cooked prunes and stuffed them with peanut butter.

But when you hate to cook, you need concern yourself mainly with only two kinds: vegetable salads and fruit salads. Of the two, the vegetable salad is the more important because you don't have to cut up all that fruit; and first and foremost among the vegetable salads is the GREEN SALAD.

It is important to fix firmly in your mind the proper proportions of the classic vinegar-and-oil dressing for the green salad. These are, roughly speaking,

1 part wine vinegar

and

2 parts olive oil

or, to put it another way,

2 parts olive oil

and

1 part wine vinegar

(These proportions are stressed here because, when you hate to cook, it is easy to reverse them, and the result would pickle herring.)

Also, if you are serving wine with dinner, you should use lemon juice instead of the wine vinegar, although, if your friends are like my friends, they wouldn't be able to tell the difference, and they wouldn't tell on you if they could.

Of course, you need a little salt and coarse-ground pepper, and you can rub the bowl with garlic if you like it, or crush half a garlic clove with the salt if you like it a lot. And that's *it:* a nice, easy, understated dressing to use on romaine, endive, iceberg lettuce, limestone lettuce, fresh raw spinach leaves, or whatever you have around.

You may also add, if you like, anchovies and thin-sliced unpeeled cucumbers or artichoke hearts, sliced or unsliced, or chopped tomatoes, cucumbers, and green onions or, improbably enough, canned mandarin orange segments, which are quite good with the vinegar-oil dressing, and pretty against the greenery.

And of course you may add croutons. On the off-chance that you'd ever care to make them instead of buy them—they're better when you make them, but they're certainly more trouble—you can do it like this:

CROUTONS

¼ cup olive oil   1 garlic clove, cut in half
4 slices bread, diced

You put the olive oil in a skillet over low heat, add the garlic, and when the oil is hot, add the bread squares. Stir it so that each square is coated. As a matter of fact, you might as well stand right there and shake that pan, because those bread squares would just as soon burn as look at you. Remove the garlic halves after a bit, and when the bread squares are nicely browned, drain them on absorbent paper. They'll keep in a covered jar in the refrigerator. Just freshen them about ten minutes in a 300° oven before you use them.

Then there are these two sour-cream dressings, which are good to know about because they're so easy.

SOUR CREAM CINCH NO. 1

Add the juice of half a lemon to a cup of sour cream or yoghurt (the yoghurt is cheaper and less fattening and works quite as well here) and salt and pepper it to taste.

If you add catsup to this, it's also good with seafood.

SOUR CREAM CINCH NO. 2

Just combine

½ cup mayonnaise
½ cup sour cream or yoghurt
½ teaspoon salt

spatter of paprika
1 teaspoon finely minced onion
2 teaspoons caraway seeds

Easiest of all, perhaps, is

ROQUEFORT DRESSING

Simply add crumbled Roquefort or bleu cheese to your classic vinegar-and-oil dressing. You can also buy good Roquefort dressing ready-made, at your friendly supermarket. Just look around.

Here, too, are three other good vegetable salads, especially handy for guests because you can prepare them well ahead of time.

FANCY SLICED TOMATOES

(*Fix this a few hours ahead if you can, so the flavor has a chance to burgeon.*)

tomatoes
onions
salt
pepper

dried basil
sugar
vinegar
olive oil

Put a layer of sliced unpeeled tomatoes in a shallow pretty bowl about eight or ten inches in diameter, and put a layer of sliced onions (Bermuda, green, or what have you) on top of it. Sprinkle a bit of salt and pepper around, a pinch of basil, a half a teaspoon of sugar, and one teaspoon each of vinegar and olive oil. Add another layer of tomatoes and onion slices and repeat the seasonings. Keep going in this fashion, depending on how many people you're serving and how tired you get.

POSH SALAD

6 *servings*

½ head cauliflower
½ large mild onion
⅓ cup sliced stuffed olives

½ cup oil-vinegar dressing
2 to 3 ounces Roquefort cheese
black pepper
small head of lettuce

Separate those little cauliflowerlets and slice them thin. Slice the onion now, separate the slices into rings, and add them to the cauliflower slices along with the sliced olives. Now marinate it all in the dressing, with a good sprinkling of pepper, for anywhere from half an hour to overnight.

When you serve the salad, cut or tear the lettuce into small chunks, put it in a bowl, pour the marinated mix over it, and crumble the Roquefort on top.

TOMARTICHOKES

6 *servings*

6 big red tomatoes
6 artichoke hearts
salt, pepper
powdered dill

mayonnaise
sour cream
lemon juice
curry powder

Drop the tomatoes into boiling water for a minute, so the skins will slip off easily. Then cut off the tops, scoop out the seeds and juice, and season them inside and out with salt, pepper, and the powdered dill if you have it. Don't fret about it if you don't. Into each and every tomato put a canned artichoke heart. (You could use frozen ones, too, but then you'd have to cook them first.) Then put them in the refrigerator and make a dressing from equal parts of mayonnaise and sour cream, with a bit of lemon juice and half a teaspoon of curry powder. Put this in the refrigerator, too. Just before you serve the tomatoes, spoon some of the dressing over each.

And so, finally, to the FRUIT SALAD, which is played mainly by ear. You peel and cut up some of whatever is available.

In summer: peaches, halved pitted plums, pitted black cherries, fresh pineapple chunks, avocados, red raspberries, honeydew melon balls, cantaloupe balls, ripe whole strawberries, or any pretty combinations thereof. Don't think you need to have a dozen different kinds in one salad, either. This isn't the Waldorf-Astoria. Three is *quite* all right.

And in winter: canned mandarin orange segments, frozen pineapple chunks, bananas, diced red apples (rind on), winter pears, frozen grapefruit sections, white seedless grapes. Those frozen grapefruit sections are handy, incidentally, winter *or* summer. You'd hardly know the difference from fresh, and they save a lot of trouble.

Then you serve this on dark green romaine, preferably, or in hollowed-out melon halves. If you're having people help themselves, you can serve it in a big hollowed-out watermelon. Or you can be absolutely revolutionary and serve it out of a bowl.

And you pass one of these three easy dressings:

HONEY-LIME DRESSING

Thin honey, to taste, with lime juice. (Bottled lime juice is very handy and lasts forever.)

ORANGE MAYONNAISE

Thin mayonnaise, to taste, with fresh or frozen orange juice.

CHUTNEY CREAM

Mix:

> 1 cup sour cream
> ½ cup chopped chutney
> juice of ½ lemon or lime

There.

Chapter 4

Spuds and Other Starches

or Ballast Is a Girl's Best Friend

JUST SAY POTATO to the lady who hates to cook, and ten to one she'll think BAKED.

No wonder. The honest baked potato is a noble thing. And like your Little Basic Black Dress, nobody notices it especially but nobody objects to it either, and you can dress it up or down.

Also, it is easy to bake a potato, because you just scrub it and butter it and put it in the oven, where it will bake from 350° to 475°, depending on what else is in there. And it doesn't dirty up a single pan!

Now, it often happens, while you're preparing dinner, that your mind is on higher things, or lower, as the case may be, and presently you notice that you *forgot to put the potatoes in*. When this happens, you can parboil them for five minutes before putting them in to bake, or you can stick an aluminum skewer or an aluminum nail into each potato. Either of these maneuvers speeds up the baking process a good fifteen to twenty minutes.

Or, in the case of potatoes that you forgot to put around a roast in a 300° oven, you can parboil them *fifteen* minutes and then put them around the roast, and they'll be done in about forty-five minutes.

Never believe the people who tell you that pricking potatoes with a fork keeps them fresh and flaky if you're going to let the potatoes sit around for a while after they've baked. These people are dreamers, for the potatoes will be only *slightly* less soggy if pricked than if unpricked. Actually, the only thing to do is to eat the potatoes as soon as they come out of the oven, or else let them go merrily on baking—in which case the skins will be crisper and harder, but many people prefer them that way. However, all this is a minor matter; and if a somewhat soggy potato is the worst thing that ever happens to you, you are Lady Luck's own tot. The butter and salt and pepper will make them taste good anyway.

How to Dress Them Up If You Care to   Gash and squeeze each baked spud and put in it a chunk of anchovy butter (butter creamed with anchovy paste) or Roquefort butter (butter creamed with Roquefort cheese), or else pass a bowl of sour cream (beaten a bit to mayonnaise consistency) or sour cream combined with onion-soup mix, or chopped parsley, chopped chives, chopped green onion tops, or crisp crumbled bacon.

Now, it's true that sometimes—say, once a decade—it seems imperative to serve a starch that isn't a baked potato. When you are faced with this, you may find the next few items handy.

SPUDS O'GROTTEN
(*A fine old Irish recipe originated by Mother O'Grotten, who recently emigrated from County Cork.*)
Cook and mash your potatoes as usual (they're best if you mash them with hot milk). Then pile them into a greased casserole dish and sprinkle grated sharp cheese on top. Don't be mingy with the cheese. Put on plenty. Bake them, uncovered, at 350° for fifteen minutes.

FLUFFY ONION SPUDS

6-8 servings

(Handy if you are roasting meat in a 300° oven and for some odd reason are not roasting your potatoes around it.) Cook and mash five good-sized potatoes, using cream, salt, and pepper. Now chop and sauté a middle-sized onion until it's tender, in five tablespoons of butter. Add it to the potatoes. Put all this in a pretty, greased, oven-proof dish and set it, uncovered, in that 300° oven where the roast is, for forty-five minutes.

MUSHROOM SPUDS

5-6 servings

You find your grater with the big holes in it and you grate four middle-sized pared potatoes. Then you mix a can of condensed cream of mushroom soup (or celery soup, in which case you call the whole thing Celery Spuds) with half a can of milk, heat it, pour it over the potatoes, and bake, uncovered, at 350° for an hour and fifteen minutes.

FANCY BAKED FRIES

4 servings

Scrub three baking potatoes but don't peel them. Cut them so they vaguely resemble French fries, and spread them out on a baking sheet. Now heat a half-stick of butter with two teaspoons of anchovy paste and a dash of salt and pepper until the butter melts. Brush the potato strips with this and bake them in a 350° oven for thirty-five minutes.

FAST FRIES

3-4 servings

Take a can of small white potatoes and drain, rinse, and slice them. Melt a little butter in a heavy skillet, then add the potato slices, onion salt (or half a teaspoon of onion juice), and pepper. Cook them over medium heat till they're brown, then pretty them up with chopped parsley.

CRISSCROSS POTATOES

(Easy, fast, and good with fish or anything else with which you like French fries.) Cut middle-sized baking potatoes in half, the long way. With

a knife, score the cut sides crisscross fashion, about a quarter of an inch deep. Mix a little salt and dry mustard with butter—allowing a scant tablespoon of butter for each potato half—and spread this on the potatoes. Bake them as usual, anywhere from 350° to 475° for an hour.

FAST CHEESE SCALLOP

3-4 servings

You make about one and a half cups of cream sauce seasoned with dry mustard and a bit of Worcestershire (or use somewhat thinned celery soup) and pour it over canned white potatoes—about two cups, or a one-pound can—in a casserole dish. Put plenty of grated cheese on top, and bake, uncovered, at 350° for twenty-five minutes.

PARMESAN POTATOES

6-8 servings

(Lovely and creamy and fattening, and good in the summertime with a barbecued steak.)

4 large peeled potatoes,   ⅓ cup grated Parmesan
    sliced thin   1 teaspoon salt
2 cups milk   dash of pepper
½ cup heavy cream

Put the potatoes, milk, salt, and pepper in the top of your double boiler over boiling water, and cook for thirty minutes. Now pour this into a baking dish, pour on the cream, and top it with the Parmesan. Bake at 350° for twenty minutes.

SOMETHING ELSE TO DO WITH NEW POTATOES BESIDES BOILING THEM AND ROLLING THEM IN MELTED BUTTER AND PARSLEY

Boil them, unpeeled. After they're tender, slice them, still unpeeled, into a skillet that contains a lump of butter, melted, and some chopped green onions. Fry them gently, stirring once in a while, and chop some parsley into them, just before serving.

Then there are SWEET POTATOES. It's nice to know that they've recently repealed the law that made marshmallows mandatory in every dish of Baked Sweet Potatoes. You are now perfectly within your rights to mash canned sweet potatoes with a little orange juice, butter, and brown sugar to taste, then pile them into a buttered baking dish with a little more brown sugar on top. You bake these, covered, for thirty minutes at 350°, then uncovered until they brown.

Or you can make

SOLLY'S SWEET POTATOES

4-6 *servings*

(*A handy item, incidentally, when you have foolishly volunteered to bring something.*)

5 canned sweet potatoes   butter
2 unpeeled oranges   brown sugar
salt, pepper   ½ cup honey

Cut the potatoes deftly into inch-thick slices. Slice the unpeeled oranges *very* thin. Then alternate thin layers in a casserole dish like this: potatoes, orange slices, salt, pepper, dots of butter, two tablespoons of brown sugar. Pour the honey over the top now, and bake, uncovered, at 350° for forty-five minutes.

Don't fret too much about NOODLES. Whatever you do to them, they remain noodle-like, which Providence probably intended. For a slight change of pace, you can put a good teaspoonful of instant bouillon into the noodle water, and serve them with lots of butter and lots of paprika. Or you can skip the paprika in favor of poppy seeds, enough to speckle them thoroughly. But don't expect too much.

As for MACARONI, the following recipe is handy, because it will stretch a meal when the pork chops turn out to be smaller than you thought they were. It's a good main dish, too.

MAMA'S MACARONI

4 *servings*

4 slices bacon, chopped   1 small jar pimento-stuffed
½ green pepper, chopped   olives, sliced
1 large onion, chopped   8 ounces macaroni, cooked

Fry the bacon bits till they're crisp, then add the onion and green pepper, and cook over low heat until they're tender. Add the olive slices, and mix the whole works with the hot cooked macaroni. Taste it, then salt it. You may serve it with parsley, and tomato salad on the side.

RICE presents no real problems, except how to afford the

wild kind. But when you get tired of looking at it plain, you can make

ROSY RICE

Substitute tomato juice or V-8 juice for half the water you would ordinarily use in the cooking. Before serving, add a little butter and a dash of garlic salt.

Incidentally, if your rice usually turns out soggy, and if this bothers you, it is handy to know the following system for cooking rice so it's dry, with each grain separate. This system has two disadvantages. You can't use just any saucepan; it must be a thick-bottomed one, heavy iron or enameled iron. You will have to soak the pan, too, before you wash it afterward. But in this world we can't have everything.

DRY RICE

Use one and a half cups of water to one cup of rice, and bring it to a fast boil in that thick-bottomed pan. Boil it with the lid off for five minutes. Then turn the heat to medium and cook until the water has apparently boiled away. Now turn the burner to its lowest possible heat, or flame, cover the pan, and cook it for twenty minutes *without stirring*.

That's the big thing. Don't stir. You can muss it around a bit on the surface with a spoon, if you care to, but you must not disturb the crust that's on the bottom. This apparently does something magical, to make the rice dry and the pan hard to wash.

Should you ever use this method, allow a little more rice than you normally would, because it doesn't expand quite so much.

CHEESE RICE

6 *servings*

3 cups hot cooked rice   3 tablespoons melted butter
1/3 cup grated Parmesan   dash of pepper
Just toss these things together.

RAISIN RICE
(*Easy, and good with anything curried.*)

6-8 *servings*

1 1/3 cups rice   1/4 cup slivered almonds
1 teaspoon salt   2 tablespoons butter

¼ cup onion, thinly sliced   ¼ cup seedless raisins

Cook the rice. While it cooks, sauté the onions and almonds in the butter till they're a gentle brown. (You buy the almonds already toasted and slivered, of course, in cans at practically any grocer's. If they're the already-toasted kind, don't recook them—add them later.) Then add the raisins, heat thoroughly, and when the rice is done cooking, mix everything together. Now taste it—it may need a little more salt.

And finally we come, with a mild flourish of trumpets, to

MRS. VANDERBILT'S COOK'S WILD RICE
6 ample servings

(Nearly every wild-rice recipe you run into calls for mushrooms—which make an already ridiculously expensive dish more so—but this recipe doesn't. It's easy, too, and quite delicious, if I do say so myself.)

3 cups boiling water   salt
1 cup wild rice   6 strips bacon, fried and
1 middle-sized chopped onion   crumbled
   (or 6 chopped green onions) ½ cup grated Parmesan
stick of butter, melted

Wash the rice, being careful not to let one little platinum-plated grain go down the drain. Then add it, with the chopped onion, to the salted boiling water. Simmer this until the water is absorbed—about thirty-five minutes. Now mix in the melted butter and Parmesan. This will sit happily for hours in the top of your double boiler, if it has to. Just before you serve it, mix in most of the chopped bacon, and sprinkle the rest on top.

Chapter 5

Potluck Suppers

or How to Bring the Water for the Lemonade

DO YOU see that shaft of sunny sunshine cutting the kitchen murk? This, friends, is the Potluck Supper—quite the best invention since the restaurant.

Potluck, of course, seldom means potluck. Once in a while, Potluck means that your hostess hasn't decided yet what she's going to serve, and, in any case, doesn't intend to knock herself out. Even so, you'll find when you get there that she's done a good bit more than throw another potato into the soup, and you needn't think the family eats that high on the hog every day in the week, because they don't.

More often, however, Potluck means a supper to which every lady brings a Covered Dish.

Think of the advantages here!

First, you need to cook *only one thing.*

Second, having cooked and brought your one thing, you

don't actually *owe* anyone a dinner, and you needn't invite them to your house unless you feel like it.

The one trouble with Potluck, when you hate to cook, is that you never can think of anything interesting to bring; and so you usually end up bringing a Covered Dish and hoping it stays covered.

It is this situation which the recipes in this chapter are designed to ameliorate. They are a little different from the usual line of groceries, and most of them look and taste like more trouble than they were.

First, however, a word of advice on how to handle yourself when a Potluck is being planned.

Beware of the entree. The entree is usually the most trouble, as well as the most expensive. So never volunteer for it. Instead, volunteer somebody else.

"Ethel, *would* you make that marvelous goulash of yours?" you can say. The other ladies will probably join in—it would be rude not to, especially if they've ever tasted Ethel's goulash—and while Ethel is modestly dusting her manicure on her lapel, you can murmur something about bringing a couple of your delectable

LEFT BANK FRENCH LOAVES

 2 loaves sour-dough French bread
 2 sticks softened butter
 1 package onion-soup mix

You split the loaves in half, the long way. Then cream the onion-soup mix and butter together. Spread this on all the cut sides, then put them back together again, wrap the loaves in aluminum foil, and throw them in the back seat of the car. When you get to the party, you can ask your hostess nicely to put them in a 350° oven for twenty minutes. Open the foil a bit to keep them crisp.

Another good gambit, when a Potluck is under discussion, is to move in fast with the dessert. You say, "Girls, I'll bring my wonderful Hootenholler Whisky Cake!" (These things must always be done with a good show of enthusiasm.) Suggesting this Whisky Cake is a shrewd move, too, because you can make it six months ago, it's easy and very good, it's cheap, as good cakes go, and as good cakes go, it goes a long way. Also, it has a rakish sound which is rather intriguing.

HOOTENHOLLER WHISKY CAKE

½ cup butter
1 cup sugar
3 beaten eggs
1 cup flour
½ teaspoon baking powder
¼ teaspoon salt
½ teaspoon nutmeg
¼ cup milk

¼ cup molasses
¼ teaspoon soda
1 pound seedless raisins
2 cups chopped pecans (walnuts will do, but pecans are better)
¼ cup bourbon whisky

First, take the whisky out of the cupboard, and have a small snort for medicinal purposes. Now, cream the butter with the sugar, and add the beaten eggs. Mix together the flour, baking powder, salt, and nutmeg, and add it to the butter mixture. Then add the milk. Now put the soda into the molasses and mix it up and add *that*. Then add the raisins, nuts, and whisky. Pour it into a greased and floured loaf pan and bake it at 300° for two hours.

Your Whisky Cake keeps practically forever, wrapped in aluminum foil, in your refrigerator. It gets better and better, too, if you buck it up once in a while by stabbing it with an ice pick and injecting a little more whisky with an eye dropper.

Another good thing to jump at is the dip and/or canapé bit. This may seem a little odd to the other ladies, but you can say—to the prospective hostess—"Oh, let me bring some odds and ends, and you won't have to go to all the bother." Nor will you, because all you need to do is pick the easiest dip recipe out of Chapter 8—say, for instance, the onion-soup-mix-avocado business on p. 84—and assemble a few boxes of variegated cocktail crackers. If for some reason you want to indicate that your heart is really in this, you can also put some 5 O'clock Biscuits (p. 81) on a cookie sheet and bring them, as well.

And don't forget about the salad!
"I've got this gorgeous new dressing I think you'll love!" you can cry. You can then collect some varied greenery, arrange it in a bowl, and bring along a jar of

PRETTY TOMATO DRESSING

Just mix these things together:
3 whole green onions, minced

1 teaspoon paprika
1½ teaspoons salt

3 sprigs parsley, chopped fine
2 large tomatoes, diced
¼ cup Parmesan

1 tablespoon vinegar
1 cup sour cream

Another good salad you might volunteer to bring is Aunt Bebe's Bean Bowl, which has a number of plus factors in its favor. You make it the day before, men usually like it quite well, and it's easy to carry—just a jar of the bean mixture and some lettuce to line the salad bowl. Don't be afraid of that three-quarters of a cup of sugar, incidentally, as I was. I thought, "This will *never* work out!" And I thought, further, "Who is *that* fond of beans?" But it did and I was.

AUNT BEBE'S BEAN BOWL

6 servings

Mix everything and marinate for twenty-four hours:

1 cup canned green beans (cut beans are better in this than julienne)
1 can cut wax beans
1 can red kidney beans, with the juice thoroughly washed off

1 medium chopped onion
¾ cup sugar
1 teaspoon salt
½ teaspoon pepper
½ cup domestic salad oil
⅔ cup vinegar

Stir it a few times, if you happen to think of it, while it marinates. Before you serve it, drain all the dressing off and pour the beans into a lettuce-lined bowl.

Then there is the matter of the hot vegetable.

To be sure, this isn't apt to come up too often, except when you are about to start over the river and through the woods for a holiday dinner at Mother's. But remember—more often than you may think—Mother hates to cook, too, and she has been doing it even longer. You can add another jewel to your eventual crown by volunteering, no matter how much it hurts, to bring your Festive Onions, though it really doesn't hurt much, because it's quite easy. Also, it is a dish that goes very well with a Thanksgiving turkey or a Christmas prime rib or even an Easter ham.

FESTIVE ONIONS

6 servings

4 cups sliced onions
5 tablespoons butter
2 eggs

1 cup cream
salt, pepper
⅔ cup grated Parmesan

First, you sauté the onions in the butter until they're transparent. Then you put them in a baking dish, cover it with aluminum foil, and set it on the floor of the sleigh in which you aim to travel. Now you beat the eggs till they're light, and mix in the cream and a dash of salt and pepper. Pour this into a jar, screw the lid on tight, and before you start out, remember to take along the Parmesan in a little paper sack. When you get to Mother's, you ask her to turn the oven on to 425°. Then you pour the custard mix over the onions, sprinkle the Parmesan on top, and bake it, uncovered, for fifteen minutes.

Well, we have avoided the main issue now for about as long as we gracefully can. There is bound to come a day when none of these little ruses does you any good; a day when the clam-bake under consideration is to be held at your own house; a day—in other words—when you are stuck with the entree for a Potluck Supper.

When this happens, consider first the virtues of

> Chicken-Rice Roger (p. 20)
> French Beef Casserole (p. 72)
> Saturday Chicken (p. 21)

(appropriately doubled or tripled in quantity). Next, consider the following three recipes, all of which are good, easy, somewhat different, and—let's come right out and say it—cheap.

ITALIAN TUNA

6 *servings*

8 ounces spaghetti
2 garlic cloves, minced
1 large onion, coarsely chopped
4 tablespoons oil, olive or domestic
2 cans tomato sauce

1½ teaspoons basil
salt, pepper
2 cans chunk tuna, plus the oil it's in
Parmesian or other grated cheese
parsley

Start the spaghetti to cooking while you fry the garlic and onion in the cooking oil until they're just tender. Then add the tomato sauce, basil, salt, and pepper, and bring it to a boil. Turn the heat low, and let it simmer long enough for you to set the table and put on your lipstick. Now add the tuna, let it heat through, and serve all this over the cooked drained spaghetti, garnishing it first with the parsley and the cheese.

Then there is this one, which will never make Escoffier,

but which is good, easy, filling, and gets remarkable mileage out of one can of corned beef.

SCOTCH CASSEROLE

8 *servings*

8 ounces elbow macaroni
1 can corned beef, chopped
¼ pound sharp cheese, diced
1 cup milk
1 can condensed cream of mushroom soup, undiluted
¾ cup dry bread crumbs
¼ cup chopped onion
dash of garlic salt

Cook the macaroni in two quarts of salted water until it's tender. Then blend the milk with the soup and add the beef, cheese, garlic salt, and onion. Grease a large casserole and fill it up with alternating layers of this mélange and the cooked macaroni. Put crumbs on top and dot with butter. Bake it, uncovered, in a 350° oven for forty-five minutes.

TIA JUANA TAMALE

8-10 *servings*

½ cup oil
1 large chopped onion
1 garlic clove, minced
1 pound ground beef
2 teaspoons chili powder
2½ teaspoons salt
dash of Tabasco
No. 2½ can tomatoes
1 cup cornmeal
1 cup milk
No. 2 can cream-style corn
1 cup pitted ripe olives

Sauté the onion and garlic in the oil for five minutes, then add your beef and brown it. Next, add the salt, chili powder, tomatoes, and Tabasco, cover it, and cook fifteen minutes. Now stir in the cornmeal and milk and cook it another fifteen minutes, stirring frequently, then add the corn and the olives. Pack all this into two greased loaf pans, brush the tops with oil, and bake them at 325° for an hour.

You might suggest to the lady who's bringing the salad that she put some avocados in it. Then make sure somebody brings some French bread, or something, and that's all you need.

Chapter 6

Company's Coming

or Your Back's to the Wall

WHEN YOU hate to cook, you should never accept an invitation to dinner. The reason is plain: Sooner or later, unless you have luckily disgraced yourself at their home, or unless they get transferred to Weehawken, *you will have to return the invitation.*

You know this, of course. You keep reminding yourself. But it is like telling a small boy to turn down a free ticket to the circus. Too well you remember the golden tranquillity that bathes you, all day, when you know that *somebody else* is going to be doing that fast samba from pantry to sink. In spite of yourself, and with the full knowledge that you're doing wrong, you accept. And there you are, in debt again, and sooner or later, you ask *them* over.

Now, at first it isn't so bad. With the dinner two weeks away, you even feel a bit complacent, thinking of the obligation you're about to clear up. But as the count-down continues, the complacency gives way to grim, clear-eyed appraisal. You realize that no one with even a rudimentary brain would expect anyone to eat what you're going to be setting before them—if, indeed, you can think of anything to set before them. You can't remember a single company dish you ever cooked, and as you look through your recipe books, all the recipes say to add fresh chervil or sauce Noisette or serve on toast points. Not just buttered toast, but *toast points*, mind you, and by now you're hardly up to finding the breadbox.

This chapter should remedy the situation. You can look at the following eight company menus with the comforting awareness that they are stand-bys of other people who hate to cook. If one dish takes a little doing, the others don't, or, at the very least, can be done so far ahead of time that you've forgotten the pain of it.

Actually, eight company menus are quite enough. If you find you are serving the same thing too often to the same people, then invite someone else instead. It is much easier to change your friends than your recipes.

You may note a certain sameness about the suggested dessert in these menus. There are two reasons. For one thing, desserts are something we don't come to real grips with until Chapter 9. For another, I've often felt it's pretty presumptuous of cookbooks to tell me to make Individual Baked Alaskas when I am already up to my hips in Chicken Pilaff and Brussels Sprouts Calypso. I am not about to do it, either, because I know something easier and just as good, like that lovely orange-cream sherbet at the fancy-food store, and the brownies I made two days ago. Or a rare, fine, immortal glass of Irish Coffee.

This is a real triple threat: coffee, dessert, and liqueur all in one, and what else can make that statement? To make Irish Coffee, you needn't fuss with dessert, dessert plates, dessert forks, coffeepot, sugar bowl, creamer, demitasse cups, wee spoons, liqueur bottles, and liqueur glasses. You merely need Irish whisky, instant coffee, hot water, sugar, and whipping cream (which you can whip before dinner, if you like), and, to contain it, Irish whisky glasses. These are stemmed goblets holding seven to eight fluid ounces. (The stems are important, because they'd otherwise be too hot to hold.)

IRISH COFFEE

Put one and a half ounces of Irish whisky into each glass.

Add one and a half teaspoons of granulated sugar. Add one and a half teaspoons of instant coffee. Fill to within half an inch of the brim with hot water and stir. Now, on top, float the whipped cream, which should be thick but not stiff. (One half of a cup of cream, before whipping, is about right for four Irish Coffees.) And serve.

Obviously, the saving here in money, time, dishwashing, and wear and tear on the leg muscles is phenomenal. And, last but not least, people don't sit around drinking Irish Coffee until the cock crows. Because it is rich, one is enough. It serves as a pleasant punctuation mark to the evening, and, because it also has a slight somniferous effect on many people, your guests may eventually go home.

Slainte! Not to mention *bon soir*.

And so to the menus.

COMPANY MENU NO. 1
Chicken-Artichoke Casserole
Plain Baked Potatoes
Fancy Sliced Tomatoes (p. 48)
Irish Coffee

CHICKEN-ARTICHOKE CASSEROLE

for 6

3-pound cut-up fryer (or equal weight of chicken pieces)
1½ teaspoons salt
½ teaspoon paprika
¼ teaspoon pepper
6 tablespoons butter
¼ pound mushrooms, cut in large pieces

12- to 15-ounce can artichoke hearts
2 tablespoons flour
⅔ cup chicken consommé or bouillon
3 tablespoons sherry

Salt, pepper, and paprika the chicken pieces. Then brown them prettily in four tablespoons of the butter and put them in a big casserole. Now put the other two tablespoons of butter into the frying pan and sauté the mushrooms in it five minutes. Then sprinkle the flour over them and stir in the chicken consommé and the sherry. While this cooks five minutes, you may open the can of artichokes and arrange them between the chicken pieces. Then pour the mushroom-sherry sauce over them, cover, and bake at 375° for forty minutes.

You can fix this in the morning, or the day before.
Put your middle-sized baking potatoes in the oven twenty

minutes before you put the casserole in, and things will come out even.

That chicken-artichoke arrangement is not only quite good, it's very pretty. But I'd like to mention here that it is unwise to expect your company meals to look *precisely* like the company meals you see in the full-color food spreads everywhere. In this connection, I have news for you: food photographers do not play fair and square. It was once my privilege to watch a beef stew being photographed in the studio of a major food photographer. It was a superb stew—the gravy glistening richly, the beef chunks brown and succulent and in beautiful juxtaposition to the bright carrots and the pearly onions. I can make a respectable beef stew myself, but my gravy is never that gorgeous, and my onions invariably sink as though torpedoed. I inquired about this and discovered that the gravy had been dyed, and the onions had been propped up on toothpicks! Moreover, that very same morning, they told me, they'd had to lacquer a lobster. There you have it.

COMPANY MENU NO. 2
Vichyssoise
(cold, canned, topped with chopped green onions)
Veal Cutlets Victoria
Fresh Fruit Salad with Honey-Lime Dressing (p. 50)
Hot Rolls
Irish Coffee

VEAL CUTLETS VICTORIA
for 6

6 veal cutlets
½ cup olive oil
salt, pepper
3 cloves garlic, minced
2 large onions, sliced thin

6 peeled tomatoes, sliced thin
½ teaspoon salt
¼ teaspoon ground cloves
¼ teaspoon pepper

First, sauté the cutlets in the olive oil until they're light brown, salt and pepper them, and put them in a casserole. Then sauté the garlic and onions in the same oil until they're light brown, too. Now add the tomatoes to this and brutally crush it all to a pulp with a potato masher or a wooden spoon. Add the seasonings (and don't omit the cloves for fear the whole thing will taste like a spice cooky, be-

cause it won't; it will just taste interesting and very good).
Simmer the sauce for five minutes, pour it over the cutlets,
cover, and bake at 350° for forty minutes.

Put the rolls in a dampened paper bag in the oven for
the last ten minutes.

Your fruit for the salad is presumably cut up, sprinkled
with lemon juice so it won't get brown, in a bowl in the
refrigerator, waiting to be spooned into melon halves or
onto lettuce leaves.

A note about rolls and bread. When you hate to cook,
you certainly don't ever make your own. If, somewhere in
town, you can get the honest, true, genuine, tough-crusted,
sour-dough French bread, your troubles are over. You needn't
do a thing to it except set it on the table with a bread knife.

Good bakery rolls are next best, heated in that dampened
paper bag for a few minutes, along with whatever else is in
the oven. If you use frozen rolls, it's handiest to thaw and
bake them first, early in the day, because they usually de-
mand a hot oven. Then reheat them briefly—the same
dampened-paper-bag bit—in the oven that's cooking the
dinner.

COMPANY MENU NO. 3
Wild Rice and Chicken Livers
Green Salad with
Anchovies and Cucumbers
Hot Rolls
Irish Coffee

WILD RICE AND CHICKEN LIVERS
for 4-5

(*Note: You blench at the price of a box of wild rice, but
as part of a main dish it doesn't cost as much as steaks or a
roast.*)

1 cup wild rice, washed and drained
3 cups boiling water
½ teaspoon salt
½ teaspoon all-purpose seasoning
tiny pinch of thyme
6 sprigs parsley, chopped
2 sprigs celery leaves, chopped
½ bay leaf
1 medium onion, chopped
½ cup butter
1 pound chicken livers
grated Parmesan

Put the rice and all the seasonings except the onion into

the boiling water, then cover and simmer it fifty minutes.
Stir it occasionally, and add a little more water if you need
to. While this is going on, sauté the onion in half the butter
till it's very light brown, then add the chicken livers and
cook five minutes. Now mix the chicken livers, onion, and
rice together, pour it into a buttered casserole, and dot it
with the rest of the butter. Sprinkle a little Parmesan on
top and bake it, uncovered, at 375° for fifteen minutes.

Next we come to the honest roast-beef dinner.

Never scorn the noble prime rib or the rolled sirloin
tip. Remember, most men like plain meat better than a
casserole, because most men like a tune they can whistle.
Show me the man who doesn't like a juicy pink slab of
good roast beef (followed by an Irish Coffee) and I'll show
you a vegetarian who's on the wagon.

COMPANY MENU NO. 4
Roast of Beef
Oven-roasted Potatoes
Horse-radish Cream Dressing
Spiced Crab Apples
(from the grocer)
Very Edible String Beans (p. 43)
Irish Coffee

ROAST BEEF

Roast the meat, with the potatoes around it, as your big
fat cookbook tells you to—probably twenty-two minutes per
pound in a 300° oven. Be sure the meat is at room temperature, too, when you put it into the oven.

HORSE-RADISH CREAM DRESSING

Whip one half a cup of cream till it's stiff. Keep on beating
while you add one-quarter of a cup of lemon juice, two
tablespoons prepared horse-radish, a dash of salt, and a dash
of paprika.

Note: When you hate to cook, it is a good idea to make
a habit of checking the refrigerator *just before you call the
people in to eat.* The reason is that since cooking or preparing more than one or two things is alien to your nature
and your habits, you're apt to forget that you did. And
when your guests have gone and you find that bowl of

Something still inviolate in the icebox, you want to call for the house pistol.

COMPANY MENU NO. 5
Lasagne Casserole
Green Salad with Mandarin Oranges
French Bread
Irish Coffee

LASAGNE CASSEROLE

for 6

2 tablespoons salad oil
2 cloves garlic, crushed
1 pound hamburger, crumbled
8-ounce can tomato sauce
No. 2 can tomatoes
1½ teaspoons salt
¼ teaspoon pepper
½ teaspoon oregano

8 ounces lasagne noodles (those are the big 1½-inch-wide ones)
½ pound sliced mozzarella (or Monterey jack cheese or mild Swiss)
¾ pound ricotta (or cottage cheese)
½ cup grated Parmesan

Sauté the hamburger and garlic in the oil, then add the next five items and simmer twenty minutes. While it simmers, cook those noodles in boiling salted water about fifteen minutes, and drain them. Now fill a big buttered casserole with alternate layers of the noodles, cheese, tomato-meat sauce, and Parmesan, ending with a layer of sauce and Parmesan. Bake it, uncovered, at 375° for twenty minutes.

You can do this even the day before, and just reheat it.

COMPANY MENU NO. 6
Sunday Chicken
Raisin Rice (p. 56)
Chutney
Fresh Fruit Salad
Salt Sticks
(from the bakery)
Irish Coffee

SUNDAY CHICKEN

for 5-6
(This is like Saturday Chicken, p. 21, except that it's curried.)

2 tablespoons butter
3 teaspoons curry powder
1 apple, chopped fine
1 onion, chopped fine
2½- to 3-pound fryer (or any 6 good-sized pieces of chicken)

can of condensed cream of mushroom soup
1 cup cream
salt, paprika

First, melt the butter in a little saucepan, and sauté in it the curry powder, apple, and onion, until the onion is transparent. Then add to it the soup and the cream. Now salt and paprika that chicken and spread it out, in one layer, in a shallow buttered baking pan. Pour the sauce over it. Bake it, uncovered, at 350° for one and a half hours.

COMPANY MENU NO. 7
Little Crabmeat Casseroles
Crisp Tomatoes (p. 46)
Green Salad with Garlic Croutons (p. 47)
Hot Rolls
Irish Coffee

LITTLE CRABMEAT CASSEROLES

for 4

4 tablespoons butter
4 tablespoons flour
2 cups milk
4 unbeaten egg yolks
1 pound fresh crabmeat
can of browned-in-butter mushrooms

2 teaspoons lemon juice
2 teaspoons prepared mustard
salt, pepper
dash of Worcestershire
additional half-lemon
crumbs
grated Parmesan

Make a cream sauce out of the butter, flour, and milk, and when it is thick, add the seasonings (the first four items) in the right-hand column. Gradually stir in the egg yolks, unbeaten, the crabmeat, and the mushrooms. Then pour it into individual casseroles. Put some buttered crumbs on top, and Parmesan on top of that, and bake at 375° for fifteen minutes. Just before you serve them, squeeze a bit of lemon juice over each one.

The rolls will heat while the casseroles bake, and you can fry the tomatoes at the same time.

And finally,

COMPANY MENU NO. 8
Fresh Fruit Salad
(served first)
French Beef Casserole
Hot Rolls
Irish Coffee

FRENCH BEEF CASSEROLE

for 6-8

(*This recipe looks pretty disastrous at first, with all those ingredients and instructions. But actually it's only a glorified stew which tastes rather exotic and looks quite beautiful. You can do it all the day before, too. Just be sure you remember to take it out of the icebox an hour before you reheat it, so the casserole dish won't crack.*)

1½ pounds lean beef shoulder, cut in 1½-inch cubes	2 green peppers cut in squares
	1½ cups sliced celery
1 pound can tomatoes	salt, pepper, flour, dried basil
6-ounce can big mushrooms	and tarragon leaves, minced
bacon drippings and butter	onion
1 pound carrots cut in 2-inch chunks	

Brown the meat—which you've sprinkled with salt, pepper, and one and a half tablespoons of flour—in two tablespoons of butter and two tablespoons of bacon fat. Put it in a big casserole. Put three tablespoons of flour in the skillet with the remaining fat, and add the juice from the tomatoes and mushrooms. Stir it till it thickens, then pour it over the meat, add the drained tomatoes, and cover it. Bake for an hour at 325°. Then take it out and add all the other vegetables, plus three tablespoons of instant minced onion, and one teaspoon each of crumbled tarragon and basil leaves. Re-cover it, bake an hour longer at 325°, cool it, add the mushrooms, and refrigerate.

To serve it, heat the oven to 350° and bake the casserole, covered, for forty-five minutes. Put the rolls in to heat as you sit down to your salad, and everything should go along sweet as a May morning.

But don't be unduly upset if it doesn't! If you forget to serve the rolls for a bit, it's actually no great matter, and if your dinner is so dull that your guests have time to wonder where the rolls are, nothing is going to help it much anyway.

A thing to beware of, when you hate to cook, is the taut, dogged approach when you're faced with cooking for company. Listen: if, by some odd happenstance, you should put together a perfect little symphony of a dinner, with no slips or absentminded moments, you might scare some of your female guests to the point where they'll never invite *you* to *their* house!

I, personally, know a lady whose cooking and co-ordination are superb, whose menus are inspired, and whose shishkebobs come flaming on the appropriate eighteenth-century rapiers; and I'd never in the world invite this lady to share *my* humble board. I'd hang first.

Chapter 7

Luncheon for the Girls

or Wait Till You Taste Maybelle's Peanut Butter Aspic

FEW THINGS are so pleasant as a Ladies' Luncheon, when the ladies meet in some neutral corner like the Carioca Room at the Sherry-Hinterland, or at Harry's Bar and Grill.

There they may relax and swap tatting patterns, serene in the knowledge that they needn't eat anything molded unless they order it. There, too, a lady can have an honest Scotch-and-soda instead of a pink-rum-and-maple-syrup with no fear of being stripped of her Brownie badge; and not one lady needs to jump up to change plates and miss hearing what Harriet said when Charlotte told her what Thelma said when she saw that awful Henderson woman at the movies with that boy who used to date Eloise's neighbor's niece.

Furthermore, someone else is left to get the lipstick off the napkins.

However, as to the Ladies' Luncheon at home, about the

best thing that can be said for it is that—like the whooping crane—it is definitely on the downhill chute to extinction. More and more ladies are discovering that with only a little fast footwork they can turn a luncheon into a Morning Coffee (with a lot of good little pastries, either bakery-bought or frozen-baked) or an Afternoon Tea (bread-and-butter sandwiches and rich cookies) or a Cocktail Affair (see Chapter 8)—any one of which is a lot easier. And when you hate to cook, your agility in this respect is truly remarkable. It is only once in a long long month of Sundays that the woman who hates to cook finds herself stuck with a Luncheon for the Girls.

This, accordingly, is a brief chapter. It consists of six luncheon menus: 1. The Soup-Sandwich; 2. The Soup-Salad; 3. The Salad-Sandwich; and, if you are so unlucky as to find yourself on the Patty-Shell Circuit, 4,5,6. The Hot Main Dish.

In each menu, only one thing takes any doing. Also, each menu, in its entirety, can be made in advance, which enables you to be with your friends in the living room until a minute or so before you eat. After all, if they're your best friends, you want to be with them; and if they're your second-best friends, you don't dare not.

First, a general word about DESSERT.

It is wise to keep in mind that in any group of two or more women, at least one is on a diet, and several others think they ought to be. If you serve them a rich dessert which you spent considerable time making, they will probably eat it, but they will be annoyed with you. If they do *not* eat it, you will be annoyed with them. And, on the other hand, the nondiet-minded ladies will look at you squint-eyed if they have dutifully plowed through the main part of the luncheon only to find that there's no dessert at all.

This poses a pretty little problem, which is best solved by a fruit dessert (see Menu No. 1, p. 76) *plus* a plateful of store-bought petit-fours (or other rich little cakes), or a dish of good chocolates, or a bowl of nuts and raisins, or all three, hereinafter known as Oddments.

Everyone can eat the fruit dessert, you see, and you, as hostess, will not be miffed if they pass up the rich goodies. After all, you spent no time making them, and, also, there will be more left for you and the family to enjoy when the ladies finally go home.

Remember, too: if your luncheon is reasonably substantial

or contains a good deal of fruit anyway, you can even skip the fruit dessert and just bring out the Oddments.

One other point, before we go on to the menus. I have noticed that it's customary with most cookbook writers to throw in an occasional well-traveled paragraph, to indicate that they haven't spent their lives huddled over their own kitchen ranges. "I first tasted this dish at Maxim's," they'll write. "And how I wished I could hide like a little mouse in the corner of that famous kitchen and see exactly what went into that sauce! However, when I finally returned to the States (via Tivoli where I discovered a *fetucchini* secret which I'm sharing with you in Chapter 33!) I did some experimenting on my own, and . . ."

Well, these cookbook writers aren't the only people with credit cards. When I was in Edinburgh, I tasted the first of many a Celtic sandwich; and I am sure these were what the Earl of Sandwich had in mind when he thought up the idea in the first place. I didn't have to do any experimenting to duplicate them, either. What they do is this: They cut good bread thin and saw off the crusts. Then they butter one side each of two slices, and between the slices they put generous thick chunks of chicken, or ham, or beef, or all three. Then they cut the sandwiches into four triangles and they pile them on a platter and they serve them.

Notice, now! No mayonnaise to make the bread soggy. No lettuce to draggle down your chin. No green olives, black olives, piccalilli, potato chips, celery, parsley, or tomato slices, and not a sweet pickle in sight. Just the sound, pure, basic essence of the Sandwich, and a noble thing it is, too.

And so to Menu No. 1.

LUNCHEON MENU NO. 1. Soup-Sandwich
Cheese-Chicken Soup
Celtic Sandwiches
Honeydew Melon
with a Scoop of Lime Sherbet
Oddments
Coffee

CHEESE-CHICKEN SOUP

for 6

2 cans condensed cream of chicken soup
1½ small jars sharp processed cheese spread
parsley

Blend a can of water with the soup, in the top of the double boiler. Then stir in the cheese spread, and keep stirring until it's all smooth and hot. You can keep this waiting as long as you like, over hot water. Parsley it with a lavish hand before you serve it.

LUNCHEON MENU NO. 2. Soup-Salad
India Chicken Soup
with slivered almonds
Fresh Fruit Salad
with Chutney Cream Dressing (p. 50)
Hot Rolls
Oddments
Coffee

INDIA CHICKEN SOUP
for 4

1 teaspoon curry powder
1 can condensed cream of chicken soup
1 chicken-bouillon cube dissolved in ⅔ can hot water
⅓ can cream

First mix the curry powder with the soup, using the top of the double boiler. Then add and blend everything else, heat it through, and when you serve it, sprinkle slivered toasted almonds on top.

LUNCHEON MENU NO. 3. Salad-Sandwich
Friday-Night Sandwich
Small Green Salad
with Vinegar-Oil Dressing
Oddments
Coffee

Friday-Night Sandwich is the rich crabmeat-cheese-bacon affair on p. 87. You can make them well in advance, then shove them under the broiler just before you call the ladies to lunch.

LUNCHEON MENU NO. 4. Hot Main Dish (A)
Beef à la King
on split, toasted English Muffins
Fresh Fruit Salad
with Orange-Mayonnaise Dressing (p. 50)
Oddments
Coffee

Beef à la King is that fantastically easy dish on p. 14. It will stay hot and good in your double boiler for a long, long time.

LUNCHEON MENU NO. 5. Hot Main Dish (B)
Hurry Curry
with Rice and Chutney
Green Salad
with Mandarin Orange Segments
Oddments
Coffee

Hurry Curry is the ultraswift curry on p. 21. It, too, keeps nicely in the double boiler if the ladies happen to want another Southern Comfort before they eat.

LUNCHEON MENU NO. 6. Hot Main Dish (C)
Chicken-Rice Roger
Fancy Sliced Tomatoes
Hot Rolls
Oddments
Coffee

Chicken-Rice Roger is the simple chicken dish on p. 20, which you can prepare any time, then put in the oven before you eat. The tomatoes (p. 48) can be prepared, if you like, even the night before.

Chapter 8

Canapés and Heartburn Specials

or Who Started This Business?

IT IS an interesting fact that people who hate to cook love to talk and, in general, make merry. When the sun is over the yardarm and the party starts to bounce, you want to be in there bouncing, too, not stuck all by yourself out in the kitchen, deep-fat frying small objects or wrapping oysters in bacon strips.

This is one of the many drawbacks to the Canapé. Most canapés take a certain amount of doing. Not only must you make them and remember to serve them, but you must also service them—refilling and reparsleying—because as time ticks by, those platefuls of appetizers tend to acquire that lived-in look, and by eight o'clock they look as though the guests had been walking through them barefoot.

Indeed, though I don't like to pick on something so much smaller than I am, it is hard to think of a kind word to say about the Canapé. If canapés are good, they are usually fattening; and they are also expensive, not only in themselves, but in the way they can skyrocket your liquor bill. The stouter a canapé base your guests lay, the more cocktails they can carry, and goodness only knows when you'll get them into the dining room. Then, when you finally do, they're apt to be too full to eat much, which is the worst thing of all. When you hate to cook, it's more than flesh and blood can bear to go to all the trouble of cooking dinner only to have it merely pecked at.

Actually, the only possible excuse for canapés is when you are having a cocktail party pure and simple, with no dinner to follow. And, by the way, entertaining in this fashion makes a certain crafty sense. People sometimes become befuddled at cocktail parties, and later they may invite you for dinner when they only *owe* you for cocktails.

If, in addition to your canapés and cocktails, you have a large tureen of soup on the sideboard, with some cups and saucers around and a plate of crackers, your prospects become even brighter. Your women guests, especially, will appreciate you for this. They will probably see to it that their husbands inhale enough soup to make it unnecessary to go home and cook dinner; and your bread may come back gloriously buttered. (You can make a triple recipe of one of the soups on pages 27-28, or you can buy several cans of any good New England-style clam chowder and beef it up with a can or two of minced clams and a lump of butter.)

And so to the canapés.

There are, as you know, some fifty or sixty thousand possibilities to pick from: open-face sandwiches, closed-face sandwiches, wee sausages in dozens of disguises, oysters ditto, corn chips, chili chips, cheese chips, puffs, biscuits, water crackers, and enough dunks and dips to float the R.M.S. *Queen Elizabeth*.

When you hate to cook, you rely heavily on store-bought items, and quite rightly, too, because many of them are very good. A dish of Macadamia nuts is usually emptied faster than the plateful of bread-rounds fancied up by loving hands at home. There are some excellent frozen and refrigerated dips available, too, not to mention tubs of delicious cocktail cheeses and boxes of exotic crackers to spread them on, and prepared pizzas you can buy from the pizza man, and bake yourself, and then cut into small segments.

But sometimes, life being what it is, and women being the

way we are, you feel that you should make something *your-self*. After all, Ethel made that good cucumber-Roquefort thing or whatever it was, and you can't get Ethel's recipe because she's coming to your party. (Well, you could, but you'd feel sort of silly.)

So you look in your big fat cookbook and find so many complex-sounding affairs, which, as you taste them in your mind, don't sound worth the trouble, that you shut the book quickly. Then you open *this* cookbook and find just a few: all carefully selected, made frequently by women who hate to cook as much as you do, and at least a couple of which may well set Ethel right back on her heels.

BETTY'S COCKTAIL COOKIES

makes about 40

Mix together
- ½ cup flour
- ¼ cup butter
- 1 jar processed bacon-cheese spread

Now shape it into a neat roll, wrap it in waxed paper, and refrigerate it. When it's firm, slice it as you would cookies, and bake them at 400° for ten minutes. (Don't bother to grease the pan.)

5 O'CLOCK BISCUITS

makes about 20

- 1 package tube-type refrigerated biscuits
- 1 can anchovy fillets or smoked oysters, and the oil they're in

Cut the biscuits in half, and top each half with half a fillet of anchovy or a smoked oyster or chunk of same. Fold the biscuits over, and pinch the edges together. Brush the tops with the oil from the fish can, and bake at 450° for eight minutes.

CHEESE WEDGES

makes about 40

- 1 package tube-type refrigerated biscuits
- ⅓ cup grated cheese
- ¼ cup melted butter

Cut each biscuit into four little wedges, roll them in melted butter and grated cheese, then toast them in a 400° oven about twelve minutes.

PARTY PEG'S CHEESE STICKS

pastry dough
Parmesan

Make your usual pastry recipe—or use a box of good pastry mix—and roll 'er out as far as she'll go. Sprinkle a lot of Parmesan all over it, fold 'er over once, and roll 'er out again. Repeat this maneuver half a dozen times, using more Parmesan each time, or course. Then cut in strips, sprinkle with paprika, if you like, and bake at 400° for about ten minutes.

CHEESE BALLS

(This is an every-girl-for-herself sort of thing.)

Combine a package of cream cheese with jars of any processed cheese spreads you like—bacon-cheese, bleu cheese, et cetera, plus any leftover odds and ends of cheese you have, grated. Then add sherry, grated onion, cream, Worcestershire, and/or whatever else you like, to taste.

Form it into *small* balls, somewhere between a golf ball and a tennis ball, roll them in crushed nuts, and wrap them individually in aluminum foil before you store them in the refrigerator.

These are not to hang on the Christmas tree, they are to bring forth, with crackers, for dropper-inners. Small balls are better than one big one, because they're gone before they get that gnawed-at look.

ONION ROUNDS

Slice an onion as thin as humanly possible. Then cut thin slices of bread into rounds, using a cooky cutter, butter them, put an onion slice on each, sprinkle grated cheese on top, and heat them slowly under the broiler until the cheese bubbles.

The next three *hors d'oeuvres* are for those rare occasions when you feel you must be teddibly teddibly. The rest are for any time when you feel duty-bound.

CAVIAR

Serve it ice-cold in its little pot, surrounded by hot buttered Melba toast. Or plain Melba toast. Or, for purists, water crackers.

SHRIMP LEAVES

Simmer an artichoke in salted water, which also contains a cut garlic clove and a drop of olive oil, for forty minutes. Cool it. Then carefully remove the best leaves. On the tender edible end of each leaf, put a dot of mayonnaise very slightly flavored with curry. Now put a wee shrimp on the wee dot, and arrange the leaves on a platter.

COCKTAIL PUFFS

Buy a package of cream-puff mix and make them as it tells you to, which is *very* easy, but use only half a teaspoon of batter for each one. You want these to turn out *little*. When they're done, slit them, fill with a dip, and replace the tops. You can serve them hot or cold. Cold's easier.

THE DIP

If you have a package of cream cheese in the house, you always have a dip in the house, because you can thin it a bit with rich milk, canned milk, or cream, and add

salt
pepper
lemon juice
grated onion

and there you are. Just keep on tasting.

You can proceed from there, if you like, and add some minced clams and a little Worcestershire. Or, if you haven't been clam digging, use chopped anchovies or sardines.

If, in addition to the cream cheese, you have some sour cream in the house, and an avocado, these proportions work nicely:

FLORIDA DIP

1 large ripe avocado	dash of Tabasco, salt, pepper
3-ounce package cream cheese	2-ounce can anchovies, diced
½ cup sour cream	(optional)

2 tablespoons fresh lemon
  juice
  Mash the avocado till it's lumpless, then blend in everything else.

Note: When you use a hollowed-out red cabbage to hold a dip, it looks rather festive, and there's no bowl to wash. On the other hand, when you use a bowl to hold a dip, there's no cabbage to hollow out. You may take your choice.

CLASSIC CALIFORNIA DIP
(in case someone hasn't heard)
Combine a pint of sour cream with a package of onion-soup mix.

NEOCLASSIC CALIFORNIA DIP
Add onion-soup mix to a good big ripe mashed avocado, with one tablespoon of lemon juice.

OLIVE-OYSTER DIP
You start, of course, with your package of cream cheese. Cream it with mayonnaise until it's smooth and thick, then add a small jar of chopped-up smoked oysters and half a cupful of minced ripe olives, a bit of garlic salt, and a dash of lemon.

Another good thing to remember, in the canapé line, is stuffed eggs. They are easy, and they always get eaten up, which is important. Leftover canapés are difficult to cope with except by following our enduring Leftover Rule (p. 32).

OLIVE EGGS
Hard boil some eggs, devil the yolks as you customarily do —with mayonnaise, mustard, sugar, vinegar, salt, pepper— and put a small pimento-stuffed olive in each egg, too.

GUSSIED EGGS
Hard boil some eggs and cut them lengthwise in three wedges (which makes the eggs look fancier and go farther). Then, when you devil the yolks, add anchovy paste to taste, or chili sauce, or deviled ham. Or you can add curry to them

and put a little caviar on top, which makes a very gussied egg indeed.

About that anchovy paste, incidentally. A tube of it will keep almost forever in your refrigerator. A friend of mine has one she's kept for six years (her husband can't stand anchovy paste), and it's still going strong.

HORSE-RADISH BREAD

Combine two tablespoons of horse-radish with a quarter of a cup of butter. Spread on thin-sliced bread rounds.

POTTED CHEESE

3 8-ounce packages sharp processed cheese
1 pound bacon, fried crisp, crumbled, drained
1 bunch green onions, diced small

Mix it all up and put it in a pretty oven-proof bowl, then bake it at 400° for twenty minutes. Serve hot or cold, as you like, with crackers.

PORTED CHEESE
(no cooking at all)

Grate or grind half a pound of any processed cheese, then mash it till it's smooth. Add two or three tablespoons of port wine, put in as many caraway seeds as you like—enough so they're noticeable, anyhow—then press it into a pretty jar you can serve from. Cover it tightly and store it in the refrigerator.

And so we come to another well-known nonessential—the SNACK in the wee small hours.

There is no reason, of course, why anyone should eat anything at this time except for babies on the 2:00 A.M. feeding. Yet people do. After a full dinner and a football game or a movie or a committee meeting or practically any other sort of evening activity, people eat.

There are two kinds of late-snack invitations. One is the sort that a cheerful husband proffers the whole dance floor while the band plays "Good Night Ladies." "Lesh all come over t'our housh for shcrambled eggsh!" (His wife is the feverish-looking lady by the door, with the armful of coats. She knows there are five eggs in the refrigerator, every one of them spoken for.) These occasions are seldom outstandingly successful.

The second kind is the invitation you issue yourself because these things are a community habit and it's your turn. If you can't move out of the community, you should make the first move—as part of your community endeavor—and suggest that everyone stop eating so much. But until you get around to this, the following late-snack ideas may be helpful. They are all easy and they take very little last-minute doing.

First, and at the risk of belaboring a point, don't forget about Soup.

You can make it any time and keep it on simmer (or in a big covered casserole dish in a 200° oven) until you get back from the festivities. Make any of the easy soups on pp. 27-28, or the beefed-up clam chowder mentioned earlier in this chapter, or combine a couple of canned soups. For instance:

> Onion Soup and Chicken Gumbo
> Cream of Mushroom and Cream of Spinach
> Cream of Mushroom and Cream of Oyster
> Cream of Tomato and Cream of Celery

(Be sure to notice whether your soup is condensed or ready to serve. If it is condensed, dilute it according to directions before combining. You can combine a ready-to-serve soup with one which you diluted, yourself, very satisfactorily.)

With the soup, serve a big basket of cheese crackers, or a Left Bank French Loaf (p. 59) All in all, this is a reasonably painless production.

Then there are HOT SANDWICHES.

You can assemble these some time during the day, and have coffee and water ready in your percolator. Then you need only to fry them or heat them at the last minute. For instance:

FRENCH-FRIED SANDWICHES

Cut the crusts off sandwich bread. Butter the slices as you ordinarily do, and use a little home-made mustard (equal parts mustard and flour, moistened with water or vinegar). Then combine

> ham and Swiss cheese
> chicken and Swiss cheese

beef and Swiss cheese
et cetera

and chill the put-together sandwiches until you're back from
the movie and ready to eat. Then, for six sandwiches, beat
three eggs with half a cup of cream or evaporated milk. Dip
the sandwiches in it and fry them in butter or in deep fat.

PIZZA SANDWICHES

Spread one side each of two slices of bread with canned
pizza sauce. For the filling, use a slice of salami, a slice of
mozzarella or processed sharp cheese (the processed will melt
better), and a sprinkling of garlic. Grill them in butter.

STUFFED TUNA BUNS

for 6

Combine these items:

¼ pound American cheese,
  diced
3 hard-boiled eggs, chopped
7-ounce can chunk tuna
½ cup mayonnaise

2 tablespoons each:
  green pepper, chopped
  onion, chopped
  stuffed olives, chopped
  sweet pickle, chopped.

Then stuff it into six hot-dog or hamburger buns, wrap the
buns in aluminum foil, and forget about them. Later, they
just need heating in a 350° oven for thirty minutes.

FRIDAY-NIGHT SANDWICH

for 4

(*You can do the mixing ahead of time. Then you need only
fry the bacon, assemble the sandwiches, and broil them.
Don't cheat and leave out the caraway seed. It makes all
the difference, and you will be glad that you were upright
and true.*)

Mix together in a bowl

1 small can crabmeat
2 celery stalks, chopped fine
4 whole green onions,
  chopped

1 small can mushrooms
1 teaspoon caraway seeds
enough mayonnaise or sour
  cream to moisten.

Then, make sure you have on hand

4 slices bread
8 slices bacon

4 slices Cheddar.

When it's cooking time, fry and drain the bacon, and toast
the bread on one side only. Spread the crabmeat mix on the

untoasted side, cover with bacon, top with a slice of Cheddar. Heat under the broiler till the cheese melts.

RODEO SANDWICH

for 4

(This is the only sandwich here that can't be done too satisfactorily ahead of time. But it's quick to make anyway, and it has the additional virtue of calling for nothing you don't ordinarily have in the house.)

4 slices bacon	4 eggs
4 slices sharp cheese	toast or French bread
4 slices onion	

Chop the bacon and fry it until it's crisp. (Scissors are handier than a knife for this.) Now drain off most of the fat and spread the bacon evenly around in the skillet. Then break the four eggs—individually—into the pan so they stay individual. Break the yolks with a fork. Put a big slice of cheese on each egg, and a slice of onion on top of that, and cover the skillet. When the onion slice is transparent and the cheese is melted, cut the whole works into four sections and serve it open-faced on toast or a slab of French bread.

Now, once in a while you may need a supper-type dish which you can prepare entirely in advance . . . for a poker party, for instance. Men usually seem to feel that after all the strenuous wrist exercise involved in an evening of stud, they need hearty nourishment. In this case, try:

OLE

6-8 *servings*

(Good with beer and French bread.)

1 pound ground round	1 small can tomato sauce
1 large onion, grated	1 teaspoon chili powder
1-pound can corn	8 ounces noodles
can condensed cream	salt, pepper
of tomato soup	grated sharp cheese

First, cook the noodles. While they cook, fry the meat and onion in a skillet until the meat browns, then add everything else and simmer till it's well acquainted. In a big casserole dish, alternate layers of noodles and meat mix, then top it with the cheese. When you're ready, or your husband is, bake it at 350° for thirty minutes.

SYMPHONY BEEF

(This is good for after the theater, should you want to slip into something filmy and cook a dish that makes people think you're a better cook than you are.)

½ pound chipped beef
1-pound can artichoke hearts
1 pint sour cream
paprika
½ cup dry white wine or
   dry vermouth

1 heaping tablespoon
   Parmesan
2 tablespoons butter
English muffins or buttered
   toast

Melt the butter in a skillet over low heat (or about 180° on the electric skillet) and then add the sour cream. Stir it thoroughly, and don't panic if it is grainy and slightly lumpy at first—stirring smooths it. Slice the artichoke hearts quite thin, and add them to the sour cream, along with the wine, Parmesan, and beef. Stir all this, then keep it hot in the same low-temperature skillet till you need it. Serve it over hot buttered toast or English muffins, with more Parmesan on top.

And then, of course, there's always shcrambled eggsh.

Chapter 9

Desserts

or People Are Too Fat Anyway

IT IS truly an awe-inspiring experience to gaze down the opulent ready-mix aisle of the supermarket, its shelves brilliant and bulging with nearly everything you ever heard of, from Lady Baltimore Cake to Hush Puppies, all ready for you to add water to, mix, and bake.

At moments like this, you see clearly how far science has come. Now if they will only hustle along with a cure for the common cold and the cobalt bomb, we may yet have our season in the sun.

I understand that the ready-mix people, through exhaustive surveys, learned that most women prefer not to have the entire job done for them. The theory is that if women realize they haven't done a thing besides add water, mix, and set the pan in the oven, they miss the creative kick they would otherwise get from baking that cake or pan of muffins. The ready-mix people accordingly revised many of their recipes, and now you often add an egg, too.

But so far as we are concerned—we ladies who hate to cook—they needn't have bothered. We don't get our creative kicks from adding an egg, we get them from painting pictures or bathrooms, or potting geraniums or babies, or writing stories or amendments, or, possibly, engaging in some interesting type of psycho-neuro-chemical research like seeing if, perhaps, we can replace colloids with sulphates. And we simply love ready-mixes.

Indeed, in the ordinary course of human events, there is no reason why you should ever have to cook a dessert. With ready-mixes, fresh fruit, frozen fruit, canned fruit, and ice cream in thirty-seven fascinating flavors, your family should certainly be able to make out.

This chapter, therefore, contains no pastries, no soufflés, no fabulous meringue-chocolate-chip-cashew-nut tortes. Should you ever want to make one, your big fat overweight cookbook contains all kinds. But don't ever feel guilty about *not* wanting to make one. As the sage has said, these things remain for a moment or two in your mouth and for the rest of your life on your hips. And you know what the doctors say.

Nor does this chapter contain any cozy desserts, like Aunt Hattie's Rice Pudding, or Emma's Apple Crunch. These things are seldom good enough to be worth the trouble, when you hate to cook. Moreover, the ready-mix people, with their instant puddings and cake-top puddings, et cetera, et cetera, have taken care of this department with admirable thoroughness.

What this chapter does contain is one cockeyed cake recipe, a few frosting recipes, and a few cooky recipes—for those occasions when your ready-mix shelf is bare—plus some uncomplicated but rather festive things to do with fruit, ice cream, and odds and ends.

COCKEYED CAKE

(This is a famous recipe, I believe, but I haven't the faintest idea who invented it. I saw it in a newspaper years ago, meant to clip it, didn't, and finally bumped into the cake itself in the apartment of a friend of mine. It was dark, rich, moist, and chocolatey, and she said it took no more than five minutes to mix it up. So I tried it, and, oddly enough, mine, too, was dark, rich, moist and chocolatey. My own

timing was five and a half minutes, but that includes hunting for the vinegar.)

1½ cups sifted flour
3 tablespoons cocoa
1 teaspoon soda
1 cup sugar
½ teaspoon salt

5 tablespoons cooking oil
1 tablespoon vinegar
1 teaspoon vanilla
1 cup cold water

Put your sifted flour back in the sifter, add to it the cocoa, soda, sugar, and salt, and sift this right into a greased square cake pan, about 9 x 9 x 2 inches. Now you make three grooves, or holes, in this dry mixture. Into one, pour the oil; into the next, the vinegar; into the next, the vanilla. Now pour the cold water over it all. You'll feel like you're making mud pies now, but beat it with a spoon until it's nearly smooth and you can't see the flour. Bake it at 350° for half an hour.

Then here are some easy FROSTINGS:

GOOD OLD CONFECTIONERS' SUGAR FROSTING

Sift two cups of confectioners' sugar with a dash of salt. Then add a teaspoon of vanilla and beat in enough cream to make it the right consistency to spread.

JELLY FROSTING

In the top of your double boiler, over boiling water, put

½ cup any kind of jelly
1 unbeaten egg white
dash of salt

and beat this with a rotary beater for about five minutes, or until the jelly has disappeared. Now take it off the heat and keep beating until it stands in stiff peaks, then spread it on the cake.

MAGGIE'S SUGAR TOPPING

Bake your cake five minutes less than the recipe says to. Take it out of the oven, but don't turn the oven off. Let the cake cool just a bit. Then on it spread this mixture:

4 tablespoons softened butter
⅔ cup brown sugar
2 tablespoons cream

chopped nuts or coconut
(as much as you want,
or have)

Set the cake back in the oven for five minutes, or until the frosting bubbles.

Easier still, you can put chocolate-covered peppermints on top of a hot cake, put it back in the oven until they melt a bit, then spread the melted mints around with a knife.

And you can put marshmallows on top of hot, just-baked cupcakes and set them back in the oven—or under the broiler —until the marshmallows brown.

The Cheese Problem   The fancy menu-writers like to say, with a casual wave of the hand, ". . . And for dessert, bring on the cheese tray, with crackers."

Now, this sounds easy and cheap, but actually it isn't. That one wedge of sharp Cheddar in your refrigerator isn't going to fill up a cheese tray. (Remember the gorgeous illustration that accompanied that little suggestion?) In addition to your Cheddar, you'll need at least an Edam and some good imported Gruyère and Camembert, to make any splash at all; and good cheese is expensive.

Furthermore, the cheese tray doesn't resemble that picture one bit, once you've brought it out and it's been eaten from. You can't very gracefully serve it again, and so there you are, up to your bustle in Cheese Balls, Cheese Sandwiches, Macaroni and Cheese, and cheese-topped casseroles. While these things are quite all right, it's rather a shame to make them from such expensive ingredients.

Then there is another point. Cheese for dessert is rather like *Paradise Lost* in that everyone thinks he *ought* to like it, but still you don't notice too many people actually curling up with it. I like cheese quite well, myself; but I've always remembered one night in a Pullman diner, while I ate my wedge of Roquefort, noticing that there wasn't another piece of cheese in sight. Chocolate sundaes, chocolate cake, and fruit pie, but no cheese. I felt pretty smug, I can tell you.

In any case, you want to be sure your guests truly like it before you go to all that expense. After all, you hope they'll serve you something you like when you go over to their house.

The Fruit Bowl   People who have been gifted with pretty fruit knives often like to serve a fruit bowl as dessert. Often this serves a double purpose, being merely a centerpiece which may also be eaten, should anyone care to.

This is really quite economical, because usually no one eats much of it. If you've ever noticed, they don't plunge for that pineapple and ask for a paring knife, or say, "Oh, goody, papayas!" Usually they settle for a couple of grapes and a cherry, and that's *it*. Whoever thought up the fruit bowl was a canny lassie indeed.

There are, in addition, a number of other uncomplicated things you can do with fruit:

You can remove the seeds from honeydew melon halves and fill the hollows with lime sherbet. (This is a good dessert with a curry dinner.)

Or you can fill the hollows with fresh strawberries and diced, slightly sugared fresh pineapple, and over it pour a sauce of vanilla ice cream beaten with a little brandy.

Or you can make

GRAPE CREAM

6-8 *servings*

Mix together
4 cups seedless white grapes   ½ cup brown sugar.
1 cup sour cream
Refrigerate this at least two hours—overnight if you like— and serve it in sherbet glasses. Good with cookies.

GINGER PLUMS

6-8 *servings*

1-pound can damson plums
1-pound can greengage plums
chopped crystallized ginger

Have the cans cold. Then drain the juice from the damson plums and drink it or throw it out. Put *all* the plums into the greengage juice (which you have poured into a pretty glass bowl) and put the bowl in the refrigerator. Several hours before you serve it, sprinkle a third of a cup of chopped ginger on top. Don't stir it, just sprinkle it. Then serve it, at the table, in sherbet glasses.

APPLE CREAM

4-5 *servings*

(*A good, easy affair to make when there isn't much fresh fruit around besides apples.*)

Grate three-quarters of a cup of raw red apple with skin on, using the medium grater. Then combine it with

¾ cup heavy cream, whipped until stiff
¼ cup sugar

2½ tablespoons lemon juice
pinch of salt.

Now put it in an ice-cube tray (with divider removed) and freeze it until it's solid. If you happen to think of it, beat it once, an hour or so later. Serve it in sherbet glasses.

And speaking of fresh fruit, berries and peaches are good topped with boiled custard (made according to the recipe in your big fat cookbook), flavored with sherry or vanilla, and kept handy in the refrigerator.

Or you can use instant vanilla pudding in the same fashion. Add a little more milk than the package calls for, and flavor it with sherry.

Then there is sour cream. Slightly thinned with sweet cream or milk, it's a good topping for fresh strawberries, peaches, and raspberries, as well as for fresh or canned peaches and black cherries.

Next we come to those smart little fruit-with-wine desserts which gourmets approve so highly, and which, when you hate to cook, are hard to beat. These give you maximum effect with minimum pain. Nor are they expensive, as they may seem at first blush.

A satisfactory domestic port, sherry, muscatel, or sweet sauterne costs little more than a dollar. You pay more than that for a good bakery cake, which is gone in two days. If you put the wine where no one else can find it, it lasts for months, because most of these recipes call for very little.

As for Kirschwasser and other brandies and liqueurs—which cost more—the solution is to get someone to share the load. Find someone else who hates to cook—this won't be hard—and split a bottle between you. Be sure you pour your half into an ugly mason jar and label it COOKING BRANDY. Then you won't be so apt to bring it out for company and drink it up.

STRAWBERRIES IN PORT

Pour port wine over slightly sugared ripe strawberries in sherbet glasses, chill them, and serve.

STRAWBERRIES IN BRANDY

Put the strawberries in a glass bowl, pour brandy over them, and chill. Just before you serve them, sprinkle well with powdered sugar.

DESERT DESSERT

6 *servings*

5 oranges, peeled and sliced
   thin
½ cup toasted almonds,
   chopped

¾ cup dates, shredded
⅔ cup orange juice
⅓ cup brandy

Mix these things together in a pretty bowl, chill for at least two hours, and serve in sherbet glasses.

MELON WINE COMPOTE

cantaloupe balls
honeydew balls
watermelon balls

powdered sugar
sweet sauterne or muscatel

Put the balls in a bowl, sprinkle a little powdered sugar on them, and half cover with the wine. Chill for at least two hours, stirring occasionally.

PEARS SICILY

8 *servings*

4 big pears, halved, with cores
   removed
¼ cup chopped almonds,
   toasted or untoasted

1 tablespoon butter, melted
2 drops almond extract
¾ cup sherry

Mix together the almonds, butter, and almond extract, then put this in the pear cavities. Put the pear halves in a baking dish, pour the sherry over them, and bake at 350° half an hour. Serve hot or cold.

MEDITERRANEAN MELONS

Cut cantaloupes in half, scoop out the meat, and dice it. Now combine it with whatever other fresh fruits you have around: a few raspberries, strawberries, pineapple chunks, seedless grapes, peaches—any or all. Stir in two tablespoons of Kirsch, mix, chill, and serve it in the scooped-out melon shells.

COUPE ROYALE

(*Just a fruit cup, but dignified with Kirsch it's a* coupe.)
     black bing cherries, pitted (either fresh or canned)
     ½ cup Kirsch
     whipped cream, unsweetened
     ½ teaspoon each nutmeg, powdered ginger, mace,
        and 1 teaspoon cinnamon, all mixed together
Soak the cherries in the Kirsch for at least one hour. Then

put them in sherbet glasses, cover with the whipped cream,
and sprinkle the spices on top.

Here are some uncomplicated Things to Do with ICE
CREAM:
You can mix two-thirds of a cup of mincemeat and two
ounces of brandy or bourbon with a quart of vanilla ice
cream, then spread it in ice-cube trays (with dividers removed, of course), and refreeze.
You can do the same thing with almond toffee, coarsely
broken, but skip the whisky. You needn't buy a whole box
of toffee—just pick up some nickel bars at the candy stand.
Ditto with peanut brittle.

And next we come to the PARFAITS.
When you hate to cook, one of the best ways to get
around the fancy dessert problem is to buy six or eight
parfait glasses. Buy six or eight long slender dessert spoons,
too, if you don't have any iced-tea spoons. Hours before
your guests come, you can fill up the glasses, top them
with whipped cream, and set them on the top shelf of your
refrigerator. Then there they are and there you are, without
a single dessert thing to do at the last minute.
For instance, you might layer

strawberry preserves with strawberry ice cream
any nut ice cream with any chopped nuts
mocha or chocolate ice cream with toasted almonds

and top them all, see above, with whipped cream.
Or you could fill the parfait glass with ice cream, poke a
hole in it with a wooden spoon handle, and pour in a
liqueur:

crème de cacao, crème de menthe, or anisette
with vanilla ice cream
crème de menthe with pineapple sherbet
cointreau with peach ice cream

and top with whipped cream.
(Another good way to serve liqueurs with ice cream is
to serve the ice cream, or sherbet, naked in a sherbet
glass, with the liqueur in a liqueur glass at each plate. You
may then pour it over the ice cream or drink it straight or
both, as you prefer.)

And don't forget the old-fashioned SUNDAE. People *like* them.

ORANGE SUNDAE

You can pour slightly thawed frozen orange juice over vanilla ice cream and top it with grated orange rind or bitter chocolate shavings.

HONEY ALMOND SUNDAE

Heat the honey and pour it hot over vanilla ice cream. Top it with chopped toasted almonds.

A-1 CHOCOLATE SUNDAE

(A good, easy chocolate sauce that keeps well in the refrigerator.)

2 squares bitter chocolate
2 tablespoons butter
⅔ cup sugar

½ cup evaporated milk, undiluted
1 teaspoon vanilla
¼ cup sherry

Melt the chocolate and butter over low heat, then stir in the sugar and milk. Cook it, over low heat, until the sugar has dissolved and the sauce has thickened. Then add the vanilla and sherry. (The sherry isn't essential, but it gives it a lovely rich dark taste.)

Now when you're serving an ice-cream affair for dessert, it is nice, of course, to serve a COOKY with it. But sometimes you are out of cooky mixes or refrigerator tube-type cookies. Sometimes you must make some.

When you hate to cook, you ask a lot of a cooky recipe. It must call for *no exotic ingredients*. It must be *easy*. It must not, above all, call for any *rolling out and cutting*. It must produce *extremely good cookies*. And quite a lot of them.

The following cooky recipes meet these stern requirements.

MELTAWAY SHORTBREAD

You cream together

1 stick butter
½ cup vegetable shortening
3 tablespoons sugar

2 scant cups flour
1 cup flaked coconut (angel type, preferably)

Roll it into two rolls, wrap them in waxed paper, and chill until you can slice them neatly—say, an hour and a half in the freezer compartment. Bake on an ungreased cooky sheet at 375° for twenty minutes—until they're a *very* light brown—then dip in powdered sugar.

ELEVATOR LADY SPICE COOKIES

(*Once, in an elevator en route to my office, I was eating some spice cookies which I had made from a recipe in my big fat cookbook. I gave one to the Elevator Lady, and she tasted it. "My," she said reflectively, "I can sure make a better spice cooky than that." So she brought me her recipe, and she was quite right. This is a short, rich, ginger-snap sort of a cooky, and the recipe makes plenty.*)

Mix together

¾ cup shortening
1 cup sugar

1 egg, unbeaten
¼ cup molasses.

Then sift together and stir in

2 cups flour
2 teaspoons soda
¼ teaspoon salt

1 teaspoon cinnamon
¾ teaspoon powdered cloves
¾ teaspoon powdered ginger

Now mix it all together, and form it into walnut-sized balls. Put them two inches apart on a greased cooky sheet and bake at 375° for ten to twelve minutes.

SELMA'S BEST OATMEAL COOKIES

(*These bear the same relationship to the ordinary oatmeal cooky that the Rolls-Royce does to the bicycle.*)

Cream together

1 cup shortening
1 cup white sugar
½ cup brown sugar

and add one beaten egg. Now sift together

1½ cups flour
1 teaspoon soda
1 teaspoon cinnamon

and add it to the first mixture. Then add

1½ cups quick rolled oats
¾ cup finely crushed walnuts or pecans
1 teaspoon vanilla

Chill it for an hour. Then put walnut-sized pieces on a greased cooky sheet. Butter the bottom of a small glass, dip it in granulated sugar, and flatten out the little pieces. Just keep doing this—you don't need to rebutter the glass bottom, just resugar it each time. Then bake at 350° for ten minutes.

Note: This system of chilling the cooky dough and then

flattening bits of it with a buttered, sugared glass bottom will work for nearly any sort of cooky that originally called for rolling out and cutting with a cooky-cutter; and it's a lot easier.

OVERNIGHT MACAROONS

(These are mighty speedy cookies, if you remember to mix the oil and oatmeal and sugar together the night before. They have a chewy texture and an almond-macaroon taste.)
The night before, mix together

> 4 cups quick-cooking oatmeal
> 2 cups brown sugar
> 1 cup salad oil

Next morning, mix in

> 2 beaten eggs
> 1 teaspoon salt
> 1 teaspoon almond extract

Drop them from a teaspoon onto a greased baking sheet, bake at 325° for fifteen minutes, and remove them promptly when they're done.

AFTERTHOUGHT COOKIES

Should you ever need cookies for children and do not feel up to making any, you can spread confectioners' sugar moistened with cream and vanilla between graham crackers.

CHEWY FUDGE-CAKE COOKIES

(These are handy if you ever want brownies and don't have any nuts. They are good as is, or frosted with Good Old Confectioners' Sugar Frosting, p. 92, or ready-mix fudge frosting.) Find your saucepan and melt in it

> 2 squares baking chocolate
> ¼ cup cooking oil (not olive)

Then stir in

> 1 cup sugar
> 2 eggs, unbeaten
> 1 teaspoon vanilla

Then sift together and add

> 1 scant cup flour
> 1 teaspoon baking powder
> ¼ teaspoon salt

Chill it for an hour. Then, after dampening your hands, form it into little balls, roll them in powdered sugar, and bake at 400° for ten minutes.

And finally we come to a few uncomplicated things in general:

PORT WINE WITH WALNUTS

The British discovered this centuries ago, and no one has improved on it since. Put a bowl of semicracked English walnuts on the table. Put a bottle of tawny port or ruby port on the table. Put wine glasses and small individual plates on the table. Pour the port and pass the walnuts.

SHERRY CHOCOLATE PUDDING

4 servings

> 1 package chocolate-pudding mix
> 1¾ cups rich milk
> ¼ cup sherry

Combine the mix and milk according to directions on the package. When you take it off the heat, stir in the sherry, and pour it all into sherbert glasses. It's good topped with whipped cream lightly dusted with cinnamon.

Also, you might make

COFFEE PUDDING

Melt twelve marshmallows in two cups of strong black coffee. Then add enough unwhipped whipping cream to make it a pretty *café au lait* color, and pour it into a freezing tray. Leave it for eight hours. Serve it in sherbert glasses with whipped cream on top, and some chopped nuts if you have them.

And finally we come to

CAFÉ CHANTILLY

Add one tablespoon of cognac to a cup of really stout black coffee. Top it with a teaspoon of unsweetened whipped cream.

To end this chapter on a high keen note, that's only fifty calories per cup.

Chapter 10

Little Kids' Parties

or They Only Came for the Balloons

IT IS a lucky thing that little children can't just decide, bang, they're going to have a party, the way grownups do, and then have it. This is one area where what Mama says still goes. What little kids have is *birthday* parties, and that's *it*. And actually they're not quite so horrible close up as they are at a distance. The only thing to fear is fear itself.

In the first place, the decorations are easy. Little children are endearingly uncritical of such trivia. If it's bright, it's swell. And eight months of the year contain handy holidays for which the crepe-paper people put out huge boxcars full of simply lovely decorations from paper jelly-bean cups to paper hats.

February—Valentine's Day, not to mention Lincoln's and
    Washington's birthdays
March—St. Patrick's Day

April—April Fool's Day and Easter (when it isn't in March)
May—May Day
July—The Glorious Fourth
October—Hallowe'en
November—Thanksgiving
December—Christmas

Always tie your Birthday Party to the closest holiday!
Then you won't need to spend time devising dreadful things
like Pirate Parties or Rodeo Parties. January can be a Snow-
ball Party, whether there's any snow or not: white balloons,
marshmallow-men place-card holders, coconut-frosting-
dipped cupcakes, white play dough for a snowman contest, et
cetera, et cetera. And in June, August, and September you
can always make it a Hobo Party—see a little later on.

Now an important thing to remember is this: You are
giving this party for the children, not for their mamas. That's
why you needn't clean the house before they come, merely
afterward. It also means that you mustn't let a mother in,
when she brings her little charge up to the door. Give her a
harried mother-to-mother look and say, "I know you'd rather
not set foot in this chaos, and we'll bring Angela home in
about two hours, when the party's over."

(Volunteering to bring the children home is the shrewdest
move of your life, even though it means chauffeuring, because it enables *you* to end the party. When the little ones
start throwing their birthday cake instead of eating it, and
before the little Bates boy has time to wreck any more of the
birthday gifts, you clap your hands merrily and call out,
"Party's over!" Then you hustle them into their coats and
home.)

The second big point to remember is this: Be wary of anything Amusing or Different! I know a fond mother who
knocked herself out once to give her little boy a gala Mexican
Christmas birthday party. Stripped tissue serapes, Mexican
hats, and big tissue-paper balloons hung around—one of
them full of small surprises. The children took turns with a
broom handle trying to knock the balloons down. But, as my
friend reported to me, there was a certain grimness about the
proceedings; and one wee guest finally announced to the
group that this was a dumb old party, not a bit like Christmas.

Never forget that children are hidebound traditionalists,
and never more so than in the matter of food. Just try to get
Junior to taste the chestnut dressing if this is his first sight of

a chestnut, and if that deep pure wisdom of childhood has informed him that chestnuts are icky.

The first birthday party my daughter ever had, at the age of three, is a case in point. I wanted it to be a nice party, a special party. So I served the three- to six-year-olds chicken à la king minus pimentos, but they still didn't trust it. They didn't eat the hot biscuits, either, because biscuits are for *breakfast*. The carrot strips were a howling success, comparatively speaking, because they each gnawed one. But the milk was a dead loss because they were all too excited about the oncoming birthday cake. If bakers would perfect a delicious birthday cake containing spinach, carrots, lean meat, and whole milk, they'd have a hit on their hands.

This chapter, therefore, contains six birthday lunch or supper menus which the little ones are apt to eat some of.

The questions might well be asked, If you hate to cook, why invite the kids for a meal at all? Why not cleave to good old-fashioned ice cream and birthday cake and that's *that*?

The answer is twofold: When your little child knows it is going to have a birthday party that afternoon, it gets all excited and won't eat its lunch (and neither will its little prospective guests, once they've learned that they're going to a birthday party). Then, if it gets a lot of ice cream and cake in the middle of the afternoon, it certainly won't eat its dinner, and you are apt to be coping with collywobbles that night. Furthermore, you may be indebted to other mamas who have lunched or supped *your* child. *Noblesse oblige.*

MENU NO. 1
(Until someone perfects a bubblegum-popsicle-peanut-butter casserole that really sings, the old tuna-mushroom standby does remarkably well.)

Tuna-Mushroom Casserole
Tiny Fruit Salad
Milk
Ice Cream
Birthday Cake

TUNA-MUSHROOM CASSEROLE
6 *small servings*

Mix together

       7-ounce can chunk tuna
       2 to 3 cups cooked noodles

1 can condensed mushroom soup diluted
    with ½ can milk
½ cup frozen or canned peas
salt, pepper
grated cheese

Put it in a greased casserole dish, sprinkle the cheese on top, and bake at 325° for half an hour.

MENU NO. 2
(The younger they are, the better here.)
Scrambled Eggs
Green Peas
Potato Chips
Ice Cream
Birthday Cake

MENU NO. 3
Broiled or Barbecued Hamburger Patties
in Buns
Celery Stalks stuffed with Sharp Cheese
or Peanut Butter
A few Cherry Tomatoes
Ice Cream
Birthday Cake

MENU NO. 4
Broiled Hot Dogs
in buttered Buns
(let them apply their own mustard)
Orange-Carrot Salad
Ice Cream
Birthday Cake

ORANGE-CARROT SALAD
6 small servings

Prepare one package of orange Jello, using one and a half cups of liquid. Pare and shred a large carrot. When the Jello is semifirm, avert your eyes and stir in the carrot shreds —also a small can of pineapple chunks, if you have some. Let it jell the rest of the way in the refrigerator.

MENU NO. 5
Fried Chicken Drumsticks
Celery Stalks stuffed with Peanut Butter

Bread-and-Butter Sandwiches
Ice Cream
Birthday Cake

(*Note:* Cut the crusts off the sandwiches, and cut the sandwiches into triangles.)

MENU NO. 6
Cream of Chicken Soup
Sandwich Plate
(3 triangles: 1 peanut butter, 1 egg salad, 1 tuna)
Carrot Sticks
Ice Cream
Birthday Cake

THE HOBO PARTY

This is the best way out of the summer birthday party situation. You advise the mothers to send the children dressed in old clothes. Then you buy a dime-store bandanna for each little guest, put his lunch in it, and tie it to the end of a stick. His lunch could be: three different sandwich triangles, wrapped separately, an apple or a banana, a penny candy bar, a sealed container of milk, and two straws. You then lead the little bums, each carrying his bindle, to the park or the zoo for a picnic. (If there's no park or zoo handy, or no car to ferry them in, let them parade around the block with their bindles and some noisemakers, then have the picnic in the back yard or on the porch.) Bring them into the house last, for the ice cream and cake.

WEE WISDOMS AND INCIDENTAL INTELLIGENCE

A big bed sheet makes a dandy tablecloth.

Any drink tastes better with a straw in it.

When you bake birthday party cupcakes, bake them in flat-bottomed ice cream cones. The cones don't overbake, as you'd think they would, and little children find them quite exciting and easy to eat.

When you frost the cupcakes, don't use a spatula. You

save time by dipping the top of each cupcake into the frosting bowl.

If you're serving individual cupcakes instead of a big birthday cake, put a candle on each one, so everybody can wish and blow.

When you write names on balloons for chair markers or favors, do it after you've blown the balloons up, and use India ink and a little brush, or nail polish.

If you're ever stuck with having to *make* a children's party cake, you make a ready-mix cake, of course, and decorate it like this: Make some uncooked confectioners' frosting (p. 92), color half of it pink, the other half green, frost animal crackers with it, and march the animals in a parade around the edge of the cake. (You can often find already-frosted animal crackers at the store, too.)

A child's sand pail makes a good centerpiece. Put a wrapped ten-cent gift for each child in it, then run paper streamers from the gifts to the children's plates.

You can make little party cups for hard candies at each plate by sawing off milk cartons and covering them with crepe paper. If you want to turn them into baskets, use pipe cleaners for handles.

Two shiny red apples, cored, make good candlestick holders.

Most children will eat peanut butter *on* anything or *in* anything. Should you ever fear your child will grow up without ever becoming intimate with a green vegetable, spread some peanut butter on a lettuce leaf and roll it up and give it to him. He will probably eat it. Equally successful, usually, is the celery-stick–peanut-butter maneuver, as in Menus No. 3 and No. 5.

You can also, if you feel up to it, spread peanut butter on rolled-out biscuit dough, spread jelly on top of it, then roll it up like a jelly roll, slice one inch thick, and bake as usual.

In the summertime, you can freeze maraschino cherries

inside ice cubes, for the lemonade. If there are some left over, they're good in Old-Fashioneds, too.

And speaking of lemonade, you can serve it in clear plastic glasses with a drop of different-colored food coloring in each, which looks mighty gay, and furthermore the little children can then tell whose is which.

Little children will often arrive at a birthday party ahead of time. They just can't wait, that's all. So it's a good idea to have a card table set up somewhere, with crayons and coloring books on it, to occupy them till the party starts. If you get desperate, you can also improvise a ring-toss game out of empty pop bottles and rubber jar rings.

If you ever find yourself making popcorn balls, mold the candied popcorn around the candy end of a lollipop.

You needn't set a party table at all if you'll round up a bunch of shoe boxes and do this: In each box put wrapped-up sandwiches, a paper cup of Orange-Carrot Salad (see Menu No. 4), cookies, a small carton of chocolate milk, a straw, a paper napkin, and a spoon. Then wrap each box like a present, in bright paper, with a name tag for each, and let the guests open and eat their lunch on the playroom floor.

The little ones think it's lots of fun to write secret messages with invisible ink; and on rainy afternoons, there are worse things they could be doing. So you give them a cup of milk and let them write with it, on plain white bond paper. (The brush from their set of paints works fine.) Then you stick around, for safety purposes, while they hold the paper close to the fire, or over a hot stove burner, and see the message appear.

Also, if they are out of modeling clay and need some desperately, you can mix

> 1 cup salt
> 1 cup flour
> 1 cup water

plus a drop of food coloring. Then cook it over low heat till it thickens, and let it cool.

When little children are eating popsicles in the living room, it is a good idea to punch a hole in a small paper plate and slip it up the stick so it's just under the popsicle proper, to catch the drips.

Also, it is nice to know that you can keep the little ones out of your hair for a bit while you're arranging a birthday party by having them stick balloons on wood or plaster surfaces, like walls and doors. They rub the blown-up balloon briskly on the wool carpet (or anything else that's wool), and it will then stick to the wall, more or less, by static electricity.

You can turn it into a party game, too, by having a contest to see whose balloon sticks the longest, though I doubt that this will ever replace pro football.

Chapter 11

Last-Minute Suppers

or This Is the Story of Your Life

DISHONESTY NEVER got anyone anywhere, or, at the very least, it's apt to trip you up when the last trumpet sounds. So it is just as well to admit, straight out, that few last-minute suppers taste as good as the other kind.

The ones that do are the good broiled steak, the good broiled chop, the superb omelet tossed off by the superb omelet-maker who loves to cook, and a very few other things which I can't think of just now.

The authorities all put immense faith in the Freezer and the Emergency Shelf, where the last-minute-supper problem is concerned. But actually, when you hate to cook, they don't solve too much. All freezers belonging to women who hate to cook show a basic and rather touching similarity. They contain a firm, enduring foundation of soup bones, flanks, shanks, and briskets, which you certainly intend to do something about someday, topped with an extremely here-today-gone-tomorrow frosting of frozen chicken, soups, pies, TV dinners, and T-bones. As for a decent emergency shelf, it's practically impossible to maintain one. When you have a few choice goodies around, like an all-prepared Whole Canned Pheasant or a complete Mexican Dinner from Old Cuernevaca, they burn a hole in your pantry shelf, and you declare an existing State of Emergency until the shelf is empty.

Thus, in one way or another, your goodies are gone where the woodbine twineth, and there you are again at quarter to six, with your hat still on, staring at a pound of hamburger or a can of tuna.

This chapter contains a number of ideas on what to do with them, and with other items of their ilk: chipped beef, canned crabmeat, canned Welsh Rabbit, et cetera. (You can, you see, have *some* sort of an emergency shelf, after all; you must merely make sure that none of the items is so exciting in itself that you eat it up slam-bang, willy nilly. No one is going to go hog wild at the sight of a can of tuna or mushroom soup.)

Entrees only are included here, because the vegetables in a last-minute supper are, as we all know, strictly a catch-as-catch-can proposition.

Desserts are not included either, for the same reason. Your big fat cookbook will tell you to "combine two delectable canned fruits, such as Bing cherries and apricots, add a little sherry, with a puff of ready-whipped cream on top." But when you hate to cook, you wouldn't do that for a last-minute supper, because it's too much work, and you wouldn't have those things on hand anyway. Also, the family might get confused and think it was Sunday.

SIMPLEBURGERS

4 servings

Mix some chopped onion, salt, and pepper with your pound of hamburger and fry some patties. Keep them hot somewhere, and to the fat remaining in the pan add

  ½ cup cream
  3 tablespoons Worcestershire

Stir it up, simmer a minute, then put the patties on a platter and pour the sauce on top.

SPEED BALLS

4-5 servings

Mix up

    1 pound hamburger
    ½ cup bread crumbs, hard or soft
    ½ cup milk
    no seasoning

Shape it into small balls and brown them in butter. Next, stir in

    1 package onion-soup mix
    1 cup water

and mix it around gently so you don't break the meatballs. Then simmer it, while you cook quick brown rice to serve it on.

SKINNYBURGERS

4 servings

Make *thin* patties of seasoned hamburger—it's best to roll them between sheets of waxed paper. Between two patties place a piece of sharp cheese and a thin slice of onion. Pinch the edges together, then fry or broil as usual.

SHERRYBURGERS

4 servings

Make patties from a pound of seasoned hamburger. Brown them in a little butter in a skillet, then put them in a baking dish. Mix and heat in the same skillet.

    1 can condensed mushroom soup
    ¼ cup sherry

and pour it over the patties. Then bake them at 375° for fifteen minutes.

PIERRE'S PATTIES

4 servings

    1 pound hamburger
    1 small can mushrooms
    1 can prepared onion soup
    toast

Fry hamburger patties (unseasoned), turning occasionally, till they're half done. Then put the mushrooms on top of them. Open the can of onion soup now, and pour only the liquid into the skillet. Then fish out the onion pieces and put them on top of the patties, cover, and simmer till the onion bits start to curl.

This is good served on thick slices of toast over which you've poured the pan juice. Parmesan is good on top, too.

MUFFINBURGER

6 servings

Mix up
1½ pounds hamburger
1 can consommé
1 tablespoon chopped onion

1 teaspoon salt
⅛ teaspoon pepper
2 tablespoons meat sauce
  (A-1 or other varieties)

Spread this an inch thick in a ten-inch cake pan. Then mix a package of ready-mix corn muffins as the package tells you to, and pour it over the top. Bake at 350° for thirty minutes.

FAST SKILLET SUPPER

4 servings

Cook half a cup of rice while you fry one pound of crumbled hamburger and two chopped onions in two tablespoons of butter. Add the rice to it. Then add

1½ cups canned tomatoes
½ teaspoon prepared mustard
½ teaspoon chili powder
1 teaspoon salt

⅛ teaspoon pepper
1 package frozen cut green
beans

Cover this now and simmer it till the beans are tender but still green—about fifteen minutes.

PATTY'S PATTIES

6 servings

With one and a half pounds of hamburger, mix
1 tablespoon parsley,
  chopped
1 tablespoon onion, chopped

1 teaspoon salt
dash of black pepper

3 middle-sized tomatoes chopped small,
  with the watery seedy juice drained off

Now shape all this into small patties and fry them, two or three minutes per side, in butter. Then take them out, keep them hot somewhere, lower the heat under the skillet and pour in one and a half cups of sour cream. Bring it to a boil, season it with salt and pepper, and pour it over the little hot cakes.

Sometimes there isn't much in the house besides bacon and eggs. In that case, you can have Bacon and Eggs. Or you can borrow a potato and an onion from the lady next door and make an

OLD-FASHIONED FARM FRY

4 servings

4 eggs
4 slices bacon
4 boiled potatoes, cubed (or an equal amount of canned potatoes)

1 tablespoon chopped onion
½ cup grated cheese
salt, pepper

Chop the bacon rather fine and fry it till it's crisp. Now drain all but a couple of tablespoons of the fat off, and add the potatoes, onion, salt, and pepper. Cook it gently till the potatoes are a nice old-ivory color. Then sprinkle the cheese over it all and break the four eggs into the skillet. Stir it constantly over low heat till the eggs are set, then call the hands.

Just a word here, before we proceed to FAST FISH.

When you arrive home in a dead heat with your family, it's a good idea to set the table *immediately*. Then the children may stop screaming, and even your husband may relax a little, believing things to be further along than they are. It helps, too, to use your best china and serving dishes. A silver bowl gives a certain *je ne sais quoi* to creamed tuna, and plain ice cream tastes better in pretty sherbet glasses.

Another thing that helps, if your husband likes wine with his meals, is to keep a few bottles of red wine stashed away somewhere. (Most red wines can be served at room temperature, so this saves chilling time.) You can bring forth a bottle with your last-minute supper, and this may lead him to think he's going first class. The sort of wine doesn't matter too much. It can be a whimsical little $4.95 bottle or a downright comical 59¢ vintage; it's the principle of the thing that counts.

RAGTIME TUNA

4-5 servings

(You won't believe this, but I first tasted this dish at an extremely fancy buffet, knee deep in baby brown orchids. This dish is probably why they could afford the baby brown orchids. Anyway, the hostess told me how she did it, and to keep it to myself, which proves you can't trust anybody these days.)

2 cans macaroni and cheese
2 cans chunk tuna
grated cheese

Alternate layers of macaroni and tuna in a greased casserole dish till you run out of material. Sprinkle the grated cheese lavishly on top and bake, uncovered, at 300° for thirty minutes.

CANTON TUNA

4 servings

1 can condensed cream of celery soup
⅓ cup milk
green pepper
celery
1 can chow mein noodles
1 can tuna

Thin the soup with the milk, add the tuna, a bit of chopped green pepper and celery if you have them, heat, and serve over the noodles.

A little soy sauce is good in this, but it isn't essential.

Incidentally, never feel guilty about serving a last-minute supper. Remember, there is a certain poetic justice apparent here. Every red-blooded American girl gets miffed once in a while when a dinner that took her two hours to prepare gets eaten in nine minutes. Sometimes it is comforting to reflect that you didn't spend a bit more time making it than it took the family to dispose of it.

BARCELONA BEANS

4-5 servings

In a saucepan mix together

1 big can baked beans (1 pound 12 ounces)
½ pound grated sharp cheese
small can chopped pimentos
small jar stuffed olives, sliced.

Stir it over low heat until the cheese is melted and it's hot clear through. Good with ready-mix corn muffins and sliced tomatoes.

Note: Never forget the virtues of those ready-mix corn muffins (which take about one and a half minutes to mix up) when you're cooking a top-of-the-stove last-minute supper. Nor corn bread. Nor refrigerator biscuits. With butter and marmalade, they make a meal seem better, besides plugging a lot of holes.

Another thing to remember is soup. In warm weather, jellied consommé is ideal, if your family likes it, because

if it's been in the freezer part of the refrigerator, it's totally
ready. Open the can, spoon the consommé into cups or
glass dishes (which look chillier) with a lemon or lime
wedge on the side. Or you can serve cold V-8 juice the
same way.

But, hot or cold, soup gives the family something to do
while the last-minute supper heats or while you wonder what
to do next.

CORNED BEEF DIABLE

3 servings

1 can corned beef	horse-radish
prepared mustard	cracker crumbs
beaten egg	butter

Remove the beef from the can and slice it into six thick
pieces. Mix the mustard and horse-radish in equal parts,
spread the slices with it, then dip them in the beaten egg
(to which you've added two tablespoons of water) and in
the cracker crumbs, and fry them in butter till they're light
brown.

This is good with instant mashed potatoes.

ANTHONY'S SHRIMP

5-6 servings

3 tablespoons olive oil	2 packages thawed shrimp
⅓ cup butter	1 cup sliced fresh mushrooms
1 big cut garlic clove	juice of ½ lemon

First, you heat the fat, in a skillet, with the garlic. Add the
shrimp and cook about seven minutes. While they're cooking,
sauté the mushrooms in a little butter in another pan. When
the shrimp are browned, add the mushrooms and lemon juice
and simmer five minutes.

Serve it on toast.

FAST RABBIT

3 servings

½ pound grated sharp cheese
1 can condensed cream of mushroom soup
⅓ cup ripe olives, sliced
a bit of chopped green pepper

Just melt the cheese in with the undiluted soup in the top
of the double boiler, and when it's hot, add the olives and
pepper. Heat it another minute or two and serve it on toast.

This brings us, logically enough, to canned Welsh Rabbit,

and a mighty handy thing it is, too. You merely heat it in
the top of your double boiler and serve it on whatever is
handy: on toast, rice, split English muffins, split-open baked
potatoes, et cetera. And just think of all the things you
can add to it if you want to! For instance:

> chopped luncheon meat, first fried a bit in butter
> sliced hot dogs, first fried a bit in butter
> crabmeat, tuna, shrimp, boned chicken
> leftover meat of any kind, plus a dash of Worcestershire
> sliced hard-boiled eggs with any of the above items or
> by themselves. (Well, your husband had lunch in town,
> didn't he?)

And you can pour canned Welsh Rabbit *over* things. Over

> sautéed mushrooms on buttered toast
> broiled hamburger patties
> fried tomatoes on buttered toast
> canned, fresh, or frozen asparagus on buttered toast
> buttered toast, then topped with crisp bacon.

As you can plainly see, when you hate to cook, you owe
it to yourself never to pass the canned Welsh Rabbit shelf in
your supermarket without adding a few cans to your collection.

Speaking of this, recipe books are always telling you to
get a can of a ready-prepared dish and spike it with something, as though the product isn't quite good enough for
you as is. This is flattering, because it makes you feel like
that fairy-tale princess who tossed all night because of the
pea beneath the thirteenth mattress. But my own feeling is
that you should give the prepared thing the benefit of the
doubt and *taste* it before you start spiking. After all, those
manufacturers have worked themselves loop-legged in their
sunny test kitchens perfecting a formula that a lot of people
like. You can spike canned tomato soup with sherry and
Worcestershire, for instance, until it's practically unrecog-
nizable, but that doesn't necessarily mean it's any better.
Furthermore, if you add seven different herbs and grated
cheese to everything that is supposed to be all ready, you
might as well have started from scratch in the first place.

Finally, we come to a few random last-minute odds and
ends.

FAST SPAGHETTI SAUCE

4 servings

¼ cup olive oil
¼ cup butter
1 garlic clove, minced

2 cups mushrooms, thin sliced
¼ teaspoon oregano
salt, pepper

First, start cooking enough spaghetti for four—say, an eight-ounce package. Next, warm the oil in a saucepan. Add the butter and simmer till it's melted. Now add the garlic, mushrooms, and salt, and cook till the mushrooms are tender—about twelve minutes—stirring it most of the time. Finally, add the oregano and pepper, mix everything thoroughly, and serve it over the cooked spaghetti.

CHOPS AND GRAVY

4 servings

4 pork chops
3 whole chopped green
   onions

1 can condensed cream of
   mushroom soup
⅓ cup milk
⅔ cup rice

Start cooking the rice. Then fry the pork chops over low heat, browning both sides, about twenty-five minutes. (Add the chopped green onions for the last two or three minutes of this time.) Thin the soup with the milk, pour it over the chops and onion, and let it all simmer till supper is ready. This makes good gravy for the rice.

FAST BUDGET BEEF

3-4 servings

¼ pound chipped beef
1 can condensed cream of
   mushroom soup

1 cup bouillon
1 tablespoon sherry or white
   wine

You might parboil the chipped beef five minutes, so it won't be too salty. Then add it to the soup which has been thinned with the bouillon and wine. (Better not use cooking sherry, because it contains salt.) Serve it on toast or anything handy.

MUFFIN-TIN SUPPER

3-4 servings

Grease two muffin tins, which have good-sized cups. Fill one with corn-muffin mix, prepared as the package tells you to. Fill the other with corned-beef hash, indenting each mound of hash so that you can drop an egg into it. Bake at the temperature recommended for the muffins.

BACK-COUNTRY HAM SLICE

3 servings

1-pound ham slice, ¾ inch
thick
3 tablespoons fat
2 tablespoons prepared
mustard

¼ cup brown sugar
½ teaspoon salt
1 teaspoon paprika
½ cup water

Fry the ham in the hot fat. Then remove it from the skillet and keep it hot—in a 200° oven. Pour all the other ingredients into the fat, cook five minutes, and put the ham back into it for another five minutes.

Now take your hat off.

Chapter 12

Household Hints

or What to Do When Your Churn Paddle Sticks

As a result of a combination of circumstances that could happen to anyone, I have been, for the last dozen years, rather intimately involved with household hints. During this period, more than 10,000 of them have sifted like counterfeit pennies through my fingers. I therefore feel that I speak with a certain modest authority when I say that most household hints are pretty terrible.

It isn't that they don't mean well, you understand; because they do. It's just that they operate on the grim premise that *everything* is a problem. If you did everything they tell you to do, you'd never have time to make the beds.

"Do your ice-cube trays stick?" they ask, knowing full well they do. "Then put sheets of waxed paper underneath them, or oil their bottoms with cooking oil." But everyone knows you either give them a good tug or a good kick, if you can kick that high, and that way you haven't any soggy bits of waxed paper or oily old ice-cube trays to cope with. Sticking ice-cube trays are not, I repeat, a problem. They are merely a fact of life, like dilatory streetcars or hair-colored hair.

Then there is the Oops!-Don't-throw-it-away! school. "Save that cup of leftover coffee to make delicious mocha pudding!" What nonsense! You'd be eating mocha pudding every night of your life. "Save those eggshells to put around the greenery in the yard!" Which is supposed to do something for it besides make it look like the city dump. Or, building to a truly frenetic climax, "Is that precious wool skirt riddled with moth holes? Don't despair! Darn the holes, then get bright wool and embroider gay flowers over the darns. Very Tyrolean!" As I visualize that moth-eaten black-and-white-checked skirt of mine bedizened in this fashion, I can see that things are rough in the Tyrol.

Often, too, they want you to do things that wear a faintly unsavory aura. Cut up that old shower curtain and put the pieces under your table mats to protect the table. Use your old nylons to strain the jam.

And I haven't even mentioned the abstruse-chemical type of household hint. For instance, they want you to buy two ounces of something like amyl acetate, which you're not sure how to pronounce, let alone where to find. This is usually for the purpose of turning the spot on a stained garment into a ring, which can sometimes be removed later by a reputable dry cleaner. (Have you noticed that they always say *reputable* dry cleaner? Where would you go to find a nonreputable dry cleaner? All the dry cleaners I have known have been honest and upright and hard-working and cheerful, their only grudge against life being that people keep trying to remove their own spots.)

This chapter contains 75 household hints, the most sensible of the previously mentioned 10,000. You probably know a lot of them already. But I'll say this for them: They all work, and not one of them can get you into any trouble. (Once, I tried to remove a small white heat mark from my grandmother's walnut table with ammonia, as some household hint told me to do. The little heat mark turned into a big white cloudy smudge and remained that way until I finally called my reputable furniture refinisher.)

1. If you have a fireplace and occasionally need kindling, save your waxed cardboard milk and ice-cream cartons, and your candle stubs. They kindle quickly.
2. When you need ground nuts, it's faster to crush them be-

tween sheets of waxed paper with your rolling pin.

3. When you burn yourself in the kitchen, vanilla will help ease the pain (apply it; don't drink it). So will a paste of baking soda and water.

4. Cellophane-tape a paper pattern to material instead of using pins. It lies flatter, and you can cut right through the tape.

5. If your daughter wears a pony-tail hairdo, give her a pipe cleaner to put it up with. It won't pull, as a rubber band does.

6. Buttons stay on shirts longer if you coat the center of each with colorless nail polish. It seals the thread.

7. If you're dieting to lose weight, use only one slice of bread for sandwiches. Cut it in half horizontally, so you have two slices an eighth of an inch thick. Makes a better-tasting sandwich, too.

8. When you sew, the thread won't tangle so often if you knot the ends separately instead of together.

9. When you or the children must take a vile-tasting medicine, put an ice cube on the tongue for a moment beforehand. This temporarily paralyzes the taste buds.

10. Even very sound sleepers, who customarily sleep through the ring of an alarm clock, will wake up if you set the clock on a tin plate.

11. When you buy cellophane-wrapped cupcakes and notice that the cellophane is somewhat stuck to the frosting, hold the package under the cold-water tap for a moment before you unwrap it. The cellophane will then come off clean.

12. If you don't own enough flower holders to take care of the summer crop of sweetpeas, you can make your own with a nail or an ice pick and half a potato (or apple). Put the latter, cut side down, in the bowl, and punch holes in it. You can also pour enough melted paraffin in the bowl to make a good-sized lump, then punch holes in that.

13. If you must remove a splinter from a child's sensitive finger, you can partially anesthetize the skin with an ice cube before proceeding with the surgery.

14. If the clothes on your clothes-closet pole show an unhappy tendency to huddle together, it helps to notch the clothes pole, at about two-inch intervals. Hangers will then stay in the notches.

15. If you wrap a once-used but not-used-up steel-wool

cleansing pad in aluminum foil so it's airtight, it won't rust away.

16. Paint your garden tools, or handles thereof, a lively lavender or a hot pink. Then your borrowing neighbors may remember to return them; and if they don't, you can recognize them yourself, and retrieve them tactfully.

17. To make your sink whiter, put a layer of paper towels in it, then pour household bleach until the towels are soaked. Leave them there half an hour or so, then remove the towels and scrub the sink with cleansing powder.

18. When your hands are badly stained from gardening, add a teaspoon of sugar to the soapy lather you wash them in.

19. When you're doing any sort of baking, you get better results if you remember to preheat your cooky sheet, muffin tins, or cake pans.

20. If you apply a slice of onion to a bee sting, it will stop the pain and the swelling.

21. You can get more juice from a little dried-up lemon if you heat it for five minutes in boiling water before you squeeze it.

22. You can make a good emergency New Year-morning ice bag by putting cracked ice into a rubber glove and tying the wrist tightly.

23. To make chromium-ware absolutely brilliant, polish it with dry baking soda, using a dry cloth.

24. When a rubber shower mat gets that well-used and un-inviting look, you can clean it easily with a small brush and a few drops of kerosene in warm water.

25. It is easy to remove the white membrane from oranges —for fancy salads or desserts—by soaking them in boiling water for five minutes before you peel them.

26. If your butter is too hard to cream, it speeds things up to shred it into a warmed bowl.

27. You can get a small sick youngster to eat more food, more happily, if you serve him an eight-course meal in a muffin tin. Many little bits of things—a spoonful of applesauce, a few green beans, a few little candies, et cetera—are more appetizing than three items in quantity.

28. If you own a shaggy dog—or any sort of a dog who sheds —it's a good idea to vacuum him frequently. Then you won't have to vacuum the floors and furniture so often. Dogs usually like it, and so do your dark-suited guests.

29. Tooth paste, or tooth powder, on an old toothbrush is excellent for polishing jewelry.

30. If you must drive a nail into a plaster wall, put a small bit of cellophane tape over the spot first. Then (usually) the plaster won't crack.

31. You can clean darkened aluminum pans easily by boiling in them two teaspoons of cream of tartar mixed in a quart of water. Ten minutes will do it.

32. If a lamp cord is much too long, you can shorten it by wrapping it tightly around a broom handle and leaving it that way overnight. It will stay spiraled and short.

33. If you use an outdoor clothesline, you can sprinkle your clothes easily, before ironing them, by using the fine spray on your garden hose.

34. If you are using pared apples in a salad or fresh-fruit dessert, soak them for ten minutes in moderately salted water after you peel and cut them. They won't turn brown.

35. Don't try to wash a scorched pan immediately. Soak it overnight in some slightly diluted household bleach.

36. If you want to lose weight, paste a picture of a pretty, slender girl on your refrigerator door. This will discourage you from opening it too often.

37. Greatgrandma did this, and it's still good: Keep a few marbles or pebbles in the bottom of your double boiler. They'll bang away when the water gets low and attract your attention.

38. When you are tying packages to send away, wet the cord first, and it will dry taut.

39. You save yourself a lot of trouble in washing windows when you use vertical strokes on the inside panes, and horizontal on the outside, or vice versa. That way you won't keep running in and out to get the places you missed.

40. A good spoonful of powdered or liquid detergent in the bath water prevents a ring from forming. You might keep a plastic container of it handy on the tub rim.

41. When you are creaming butter and sugar together, it's a good idea to rinse the bowl with boiling water first. They'll cream faster.

42. If it's important to you to get walnut meats out whole, soak the nuts overnight in salt water before you crack them.

43. If your candles are too small for the candleholders, and wobble, you can remedy it with modeling clay. Or dip

the candle ends in hot water, then press them down firmly.

44. It is handy to keep a soft powder puff in the flour bin, for dusting cake pans.

45. If your veils or lace collars get that tired look, you can crisp them by ironing them between two sheets of waxed paper.

46. When you oil your sewing machine, remember to sew through a blotter several times before you sew through your material. The blotter will soak up the excess oil.

47. When you have several sizes of beds in the house, it's wise to settle on one particular type of sheet for each: Stripes for Junior, pastels for Sis, plain white for Ma and Pa. That way there is no mussing up the linen shelf to find the right one.

48. As nearly everyone knows, nail-polish remover gets adhesive-tape marks off with speed and ease.

49. Your bed linen smells good if you keep your supply of toilet soap stuck here and there in the linen closet. This has an additional advantage: You never seem to run out of soap, because another bar is always lurking somewhere if you hunt long enough.

50. If you have polished floors in the family, as well as small children or elderly people, it is a good idea to paste strips of adhesive tape on the bottoms of shoes. It saves bruises and even broken hips.

51. It saves you considerable walking if you'll spend a dollar and get at least two more measuring cups and two more sets of measuring spoons. Then keep a cup in the flour bin and one in the sugar bin. Keep a set of spoons in the baking-powder can, or in the coffee can, or wherever you use them the most.

52. If someone in the family is sick in bed and can't sit up, he can drink more easily from a teapot spout.

53. You can make a changing picture gallery for a child's room by stretching a length of stout twine across a wall and affixing prints or magazine cutouts with paper clips. It's a good way to encourage an early interest in good pictures.

54. It's helpful to maintain a lost-and-found department at home. Reserve a shelf or a deep drawer where you put all out-of-place objects, from catchers' mitts to cigar lighters. Saves aimless looking for everyone, and keeps the clutter in one place.

55. When you take a gift to a baby shower, it's a nice idea

to wrap it in a diaper and fasten it with a couple of pastel diaper pins.

56. You can remove rust stains from a sink or tub by rubbing them with a little kerosene.

57. Should something catch fire in your oven, sprinkle it lavishly with salt or baking soda. It stops the flame and smoke immediately.

58. If you are pounding a noisy typewriter when someone is trying to sleep in the next room, you'd better put a folded bath towel under it. It makes it quieter.

59. When you're starting for town and notice that your hem has come undone, you can fix it temporarily with cellophane tape. Easier than pins.

60. Put a strip of luminous paint around your flashlight handle, and you'll be able to see it easily in the dark—which is when you usually need it.

61. If you twist your coat hangers up sharply at both ends, they won't shed your slips, nightgowns, and sun dresses.

62. Your sewing needles slide easily and never rust if you keep them stuck in a bar of soap in your sewing box.

63. When you cook eggs in the shell, put a big teaspoon of salt in the water. Then the shells won't crack.

64. And speaking of salt, never double it when you double a recipe. Use only half again as much, then taste.

65. Keep your spices in alphabetical order on the shelf, and always put them back again in the same place.

66. If a blanket or a quilt is too short, sew a couple of feet of matching sateen to the bottom of it, for tuck-in purposes.

67. A ten-cent embroidery hoop is handy for removing stains by the boiling-hot-water method. It will hold the material taut while you pour on the water.

68. When dark wood furniture is scratched, a cut walnut meat, rubbed on the scratch, will restore the color very nicely.

69. You can remove candle wax from wood very easily with lighter fluid on a soft cloth.

70. If you like only a taste of garlic in a stew, put the garlic clove in a tea ball. Then you can easily find it and remove it.

71. You can use colorless nail polish for emergency glue.

72. Add a tablespoon of cooking oil, or margarine, to the water you cook spaghetti or noodles in, and it won't be so eager to boil over.

73. If the whipping cream looks as though it's not going to

whip, add three or four drops of lemon juice or a bit of plain gelatine powder to it, and it probably will.

74. Shoe bags are handy for many things besides shoes. You can hang one on the back of the cellar door for furniture polish, dustcloths, et cetera. And you can hang one over the back seat of the car for a family trip, to hold toys, Kleenex, maps, dark glasses, et cetera.

75. You can always find your car quickly—on the street or in a huge parking lot—if you'll keep a bright pennant tied to the radio aerial. Before you leave the car, run the aerial up to its full height.

Chapter 13

Good Cooksmanship

or How to Talk a Good Fight

NOW ONCE in a while you'll find yourself in a position where you have to talk about cooking. This is usually a sitting-down position with other ladies hemming you in so you can't get away.

Actually, your cooking is a personal thing, like your sex life, and it shouldn't be the subject of general conversation. But women who love to cook often love to talk about it, too, and if you're going to make any sort of showing at all, there are several points to keep in mind.

For instance, words.

Never say "fry" if you don't mean "deep-fat fry." You can say

>"pan fry"
>"pan broil"
>"sauté"

"brown in butter"
"sizzle in butter"

or you may go all the way and say "cook it *à la pôele*," which is a French phrase meaning "stew in butter at such a low temperature that the object is cooked before it starts to brown." But "fry" means the way you would cook doughnuts, if you ever did, which you don't, because you can buy perfectly lovely doughnuts all made.

(The boys behind the counter at Joe's Diner aren't aware of these distinctions, of course, and if you ask them to sauté you an egg, or cook one *à la pôele*, there's no telling what sort of an *oeuf* you'd get. But you are not down at Joe's Diner.)

Similarly, if you can possibly avoid it, don't say "onions." Say "shallots," even though you wouldn't know one if you saw one. This gives standing to a recipe that otherwise wouldn't have much. (The same thing is true of "hamburger" versus "ground round" or "ground sirloin." Never say "hamburger," even if you mean "hamburger.") You're on safe territory if anyone calls you on the shallot business, too, because shallot also means a small green onion, as well as some distant and exotic relative of the onion family, so don't worry a bit.

Another one is "cooking sherry." Just say "sherry." Actually, cooking sherry is quite satisfactory for your modest purposes in most hot cooked entrees. It is cheaper to use, too, because you don't nip as you cook, and, moreover, it saves you on salt. But I'm warning you, the cooking buffs will raise their eyebrows. And while we're at it, you might glance over the following greatly abbreviated list:

Naughty Words	*Good Words*
crisp	crispy
hot	piping hot
cold	chilled
put it in the oven	pop in the oven
it tastes good with …	it's a good foil for …
light brown	golden
hard-boiled	hard-cooked
filling	rib-sticking
top with bacon	garnish with crispy bacon curls

This brings us to another related department, and it is a good thing it does. You've no idea how hard it is to organize a cookbook, with all the different things in it. Next time, I'm going to write a hair-pants Western with just a horse and a hero.

However, the department we now find ourselves in is FANCY GARNISHES, and those mad gay touches that are yours alone. These are the things you see in cookbooks and magazines that have you thinking, "Now that's a cute idea; I ought to *do* that," but you never remember to.

Well, here they are again. I must emphasize, though, that things that seem mad and gay to us who hate to cook are probably pretty ho-hum to the people who love to. You see, when you hate to cook, you are singularly unobservant where cooking and food are concerned. You're also easily impressed; and if you ever do anything so foreign to your nature as floating a lemon slice on black bean soup, you talk about it for weeks afterward.

Well, a lemon slice isn't the only thing you can float on soup.

There's popcorn. Plain movie popcorn or cheese popcorn. It looks pretty and it's easier than croutons.

Then there are chopped walnuts, pecans, or toasted almonds, any one of which is good on cream of chicken or celery soup.

There's also chopped raw celery or green pepper or green onion tops for any sort of soup that needs some additional crispness.

Then there are fancy garnishes in general.

For instance, with any sort of melon you can serve a bowl of chopped crystallized ginger or powdered ginger.

You can garnish nearly any meat, hot or cold, with chutneyed peach halves. You brush the fresh or canned peach halves with melted butter, put them in a 350° oven for ten minutes, then fill the halves with chutney and heat them *another* five minutes.

And to garnish fish, you can dip small bunches of white seedless grapes first in lemon juice or egg white and then in granulated sugar, dry them on a rack, and scatter them around the platter.

Then, if you've bought some frozen chicken pies, you can stud their tops thickly with almonds (blanched but not toasted, because that'll happen while the pies bake) before you put the pies in the oven.

Should you ever be so foolish as to make cream-cheese

balls for a canapé, you may stick thin pretzel sticks into them instead of toothpicks. That way the whole thing gets eaten, and you don't have your ash trays overflowing with toothpicks. (This works just as well, of course, with cubed processed loaf cheese.)

Speaking of canapés, a stack of small Mexican tin plates is a good thing to have around. These aren't for the guests' sake, exactly, but for yours. When someone is juggling a drink and a cigarette and a dip-loaded chip, it can be hard on the sofa. The tin plates won't break, as your bread-and-butter ones will, and they look a little special and festive.

This is as good a place as any to digress briefly into the gay mad aspects of the *container* department, or, what you serve things *in*. For instance, the clever hostess often serves her cookies in a brandy snifter! This would seem to leave her the cooky jar to serve her brandy in, but then a lively party is probably what she's after.

You may use tall beer glasses for your parfaits, too. Or middle-sized brandy snifters. Or ordinary water goblets. The only thing to be careful of here is to make sure you have a fine complete glassware service, containing parfait glasses you *could* have used. Otherwise you just look terribly valiant.

Then there are napkin rings. The ordinary person puts napkins in them, but the clever hostess has bottoms put in hers and uses them for cigarette cups. Or instead of serving a liqueur in her elongated liqueur glasses, she puts one or two little flowers in them, like hyacinths or pansies, and puts them between each pair of place settings, instead of having one floral centerpiece. This, of course, uses up her liqueur glasses, but we can assume that she's serving Irish Coffee.

However, this is far too big a field to cover in the small space available here. To sum up: When you are looking for something to put something in, think of an *unlikely* object to put it in—jam in the eggcups, flowers in the chamberpot, bats in the bird cage—and then *do* it.

And so, back to food, and conversations about it. There are four handy words to remember: OF COURSE I ALWAYS . . . This is your lead-in for any of those little touches you want to get across. Never cry, "Girls! I tried the darnedest thing the other day, and it tasted just marvelous! What I did was . . ." No, you understate it, you throw it away, with "Of course, I always mix my dry mustard with white wine" and if you're among people who'll believe anything, you can

substitute champagne for white wine, for this is highly re-
garded in certain circles I don't belong to.

The big thing is to remember those four little words, OF
COURSE I ALWAYS . . .

. . . add a quarter of a cup of sesame seeds to my sage-
onion chicken dressing

. . . drop a couple of chocolate bits into my demitasse
for a good mocha taste

. . . dip fish and chops in biscuit mix or pancake flour
before I pan broil them

. . . brush steaks or chops with soy sauce before I broil
them

. . . add some tarragon or savory to my scrambled eggs

. . . add a little oregano to the garlic in my garlic bread

. . . add a little chervil to my ordinary biscuit mix

. . . add a little brandy to my pumpkin pie

. . . put a little grated orange peel in my cranberry sauce

. . . blend chopped parsley and a dash of lemon juice
with butter and put a dollop of it on broiled steaks

. . . put a little red wine in my onion soup

. . . fatigue my lettuce.

This last, incidentally, is a nice gambit in conversations
of this sort, because chances are good that someone will ask
you what it means. It means to toss your salad greens with
just a drop or two of oil—so that each leaf gets a micro-
scopically thin coating—*before* you add your salad dressing.
For some reason, it makes the greenery crisper.

Now, there is one more thing we must consider in this
chapter: THE SPECIALTY.

These days it is important to have a specialty, because you
never can tell on what bright sunny morning you may wake
up and discover that you are a celebrity. Perhaps you were
the eleven-billionth person to go through the Holland Tun-
nel, or maybe you had ten children in two years, all quin-
tuplets.

No matter. The reporters will be around, and the second
thing they'll ask you for, after your measurements, is your
Kitchen Specialty. You owe it to yourself and to your public
to have something on tap besides tuna sandwiches.

"*. . . Miss Sugar Belle, 37-22-35, star of the current Broad-
way hit,* Holler Down a Rain Barrel, *writer, producer, and
star of her own daily TV show, author of the current best
seller* Wheee for Me!, *wife of handsome TV tenor Vic Ri-*

cotta, and mother of four strapping teen-age boys, was inter-viewed in the rambling oak-beamed sewing room of her rambling oak-beamed farmhouse in Connecticut.

"My, yes, I always design and make my own clothes," she told this reporter, "as well as breeding Bedlingtons and doing all the electrical repairs around the place."

"But as busy as you are, Miss Belle," we asked, "how do you find time to keep that big good-looking husband of yours happy?"

Sugar Belle twinkled that famous Sugar Belle twinkle, got up, and moved out to the rambling oak-beamed kitchen.

"Why, honey child," she said, "I just whomp him up a batch of my little ole Cotton-pickin' Jam Tarts!"

COTTON-PICKIN' JAM TARTS

4½ oz. cream cheese   1 cup flour
½ cup butter   jelly or preserves

Sugar Belle melts her butter, blends it with the cheese, and stirs in the flour to make a nice smooth dough. Then she puts it in the freezing compartment for about an hour, until it's firm. Next, she nips little pieces off, about the size of golf balls, rolls them out, trims them into squares, and puts a tea-spoon of jelly on each. (If you wonder why Sugar Belle doesn't just roll the whole thing out and cut it into squares, it is because the dough is hard to handle that way.) Then she folds them into triangles, seals the edges with a floured fork, and bakes them on a greased cooky sheet at 450° until they're brown, which is from ten to fifteen minutes. And when she puts a big plateful of these in front of her husband, you just ought to see his face light up!

You see, the recipe for your specialty needn't be compli-cated. In fact, it better hadn't be, because there is always that off-chance that someday you might have to demonstrate. It just needs to be good and a little bit interesting, that's all. Any of the following four recipes would work out all right for you, too.

SUGAR BELLE'S RYE DROP CAKES

(And believe me, everybody in Sugar Belle's family gets up early for these.)

1 egg
1 teaspoon soda
1 cup buttermilk

1 cup rye flour
½ cup white flour
pinch of salt
deep fat for frying

She beats that egg with enthusiasm. Then she mixes the soda with the buttermilk till it fuzzes up. Deftly, she adds this to the egg, then sifts the flours and salt, and mixes everything together. Finally, she drops spoonfuls of it into hot fat—at doughnut temperature—and lets them bob around till they're brown. Then she serves them with butter and individual saucers of maple syrup to dunk them in.

When Sugar Belle is having some famous directors and writers and everybody over for an *intime* after-the-theater supper, she loves to serve

SUGAR BELLE'S SOUR CREAM MUSHROOMS
4-5 servings

4 cups mushrooms, fatly
  sliced
3 tablespoons butter

1 cup sour cream
salt, pepper

She sautés the mushrooms in a skillet. When they are *barely* tender, she adds the sour cream and cooks it very slowly, or else it might curdle up and embarrass her no end. When the sauce has thickened, she adds the salt and pepper and serves it on toast.

Sugar Belle is a great girl for jam, too, and with all those growing boys—*well!*

SUGAR BELLE'S APRICOT-BANANA JAM

6 cups mashed raw apricots
1¼ cups mashed bananas
14 cups sugar
    Juice of 1 orange and 1 lemon if you
    want a somewhat thinner jam

1 bottle Certo
1 tablespoon butter
pinch of salt

She brings the fruit, sugar, and salt to a rollicking full boil and keeps it that way for a minute while she stirs it constantly. Then she adds the butter, takes the pot off the burner, stirs in the Certo, skims it, pours it into jars, and pours on the paraffin.

She has one more specialty, too, which she'll carry on about for hours if you let her. Says it's good by itself and tremendous with barbecued steak, chicken, or chops. She calls it her own

HELLZAPOPPIN CHEESE RICE

6 servings

4 cups rice, cooked
4 eggs
2 tablespoons minced onion
1 tablespoon Worcestershire
2 teaspoons salt
1 pound grated sharp
  Cheddar

small pinch each of thyme
  and marjoram
1 package chopped, cooked
  frozen spinach
1 cup milk
4 tablespoons melted butter

She beats the eggs till they're light. Then she adds the milk and all the seasonings. Finally, she folds in the cheese, spinach, and rice, and pours the whole works into a greased casserole. After she pours the melted butter over it, she sets it in a 375° oven to bake for thirty-five minutes and she takes off her apron.

Understand now—you and Sugar Belle needn't actually *make* these things. Unless you are absolutely up a stump and the chips are down, you merely need to *talk* about making them. For, while they're all good, and easy, still it is more trouble to make them than not to make them; and my feelings will not be a bit hurt if you don't. I will understand.

I never thrust my nose into other men's porridge. It is no bread and butter of mine; every man for himself, and God for us all.

—Miguel de Cervantes

Equivalents, Et Cetera

or Dreary Details That You Certainly Have No Intention of Remembering

THERE ARE many more interesting things to fill your mind with than items like these. So just make a mental note that they are here, then consult these pages when it's necessary.

WHAT EQUALS WHAT

3 teaspoons = 1 tablespoon
1 fluid ounce = 2 tablespoons
¼ cup = 4 tablespoons
⅓ cup = 5 tablespoons plus 1 teaspoon
1 cup = ½ pint
2 cups = 1 pint
4 cups = 1 quart
3 small eggs = 2 large eggs
1 square chocolate = 1 ounce
¼ pound butter = ½ cup
1 pound shortening = 2½ cups
1 medium lemon = 3 tablespoons juice
1 medium orange = 6 to 8 tablespoons juice
1 grated orange rind = 1 tablespoon

WHAT SUBSTITUTES FOR WHAT *

3½ tablespoons cocoa plus 1 tablespoon fat or oil
= 1 square bitter chocolate
1½ tablespoons vinegar plus enough sweet
cream to fill 1 cup; let
it stand a few minutes = 1 cup sour cream
1 cup undiluted canned milk
plus 1 tablespoon vinegar; let
it stand a few minutes = 1 cup sour cream
½ cup canned milk, ½ cup water,
plus 1 tablespoon vinegar; let it
stand a few minutes = 1 cup buttermilk or sour milk
1 or 2 tablespoons vinegar plus enough
sweet milk to fill the
cup; let it stand a
few minutes = 1 cup buttermilk or sour milk

1 teaspoon baking soda plus 2 teaspoons
    cream of tartar plus
    1 teaspoon cornstarch = baking powder
    (use 2 teaspoons per cup of flour)
1 cup vegetable shortening
    plus ½ teaspoon salt = 1 cup butter (for baking only)
1 cup sifted all-purpose flour
    less 2 tablespoons = 1 cup cake flour

VARIOUS TRICKY INGREDIENTS IN GENERAL

1 cup raw rice = about 3½ cups cooked
1 cup raw wild rice = 3½ to 4 cups cooked
Macaroni doubles itself
Noodles only grow a third
1¼ pound unshelled walnuts = about 2 cups chopped
    walnuts
2 cups grated cheese, firmly packed = ½ pound
1 cup (½ pint) whipping cream = about 2¼ cups, whipped

ABOUT CANS

The general rule is this: Whatever size can the recipe calls
for, you can't find it. Therefore, it is often handy to know
just *how much* a particular can size contains.

Ordinary small tuna or minced
    clam can (6½ to 7 ounces) = just under 1 cup
Ordinary soup can size
    (10½ to 12 ounces) = about 1¼ cups
Slightly larger size,
    approximately 1 pound,
    give or take an ounce,
    and known as #303 = about 2 cups
Larger still, approximately
    20 ounces, and known as
    #2 size (but you don't
    see these too often now) = about 2½ cups
Larger still, 29 ounces
    (known as #2½) = about 3½ cups

* These are all emergency measures. Your finished product won't
be quite as good as if you had used what the recipe called for,
but it will be adequate.

Index

138